1 Space Camp Florida Welcomes ...

1 ▶ American crosswords

a *Complete the crossword.*

1 American money
2 The British write 'programme'.
3 The British say 'form' or 'class'.
4 When you go to a new country and visit lots of places there, you ...
5 Americans who speak Spanish at home
6 A party where you cook and eat outside
7 You'll find one outside lots of US buildings.

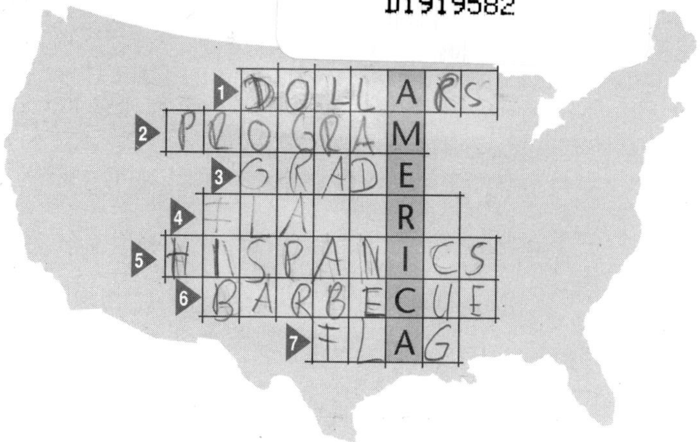

b *This time write the clues.*

1 An orange is a ...
2 A crocodile that lives in Florida.
3 Men who fly into space.
4 A town with theme parks in Florida.
5 Florida is also called the ... State
6 The landscape where the alligators swim.
7 The sand area next to the sea.

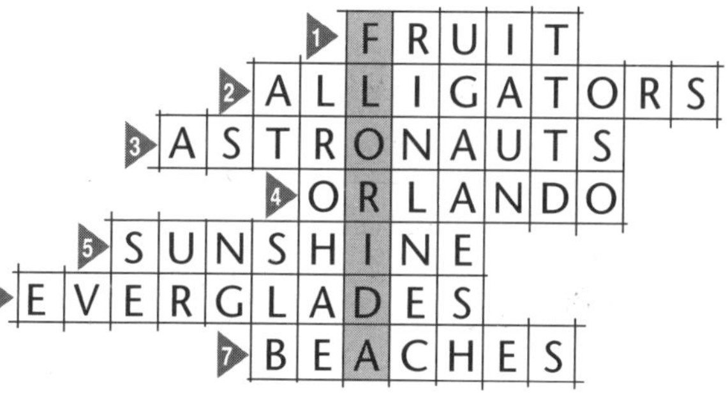

▶▶▶ NOW YOU

Make your own crossword. Choose the words and write the clues.

1 COMPUTER
2 SPACE SHUTTLE
3 MARS

(USA)

1 A machine with a keyboard and a Screen
2 A space ship which can be used many times.
3 The red planet.

p. 9

2 ▶ Telephone language

a *Match these phrases.*

- Wer ist dran?
- Einen Moment, bitte.
- Kann ich bitte mit ... sprechen?
- Kann ich etwas ausrichten?
- Hier spricht ...
- Ich rufe später zurück.
- Ich habe die falsche Nummer gewählt.
- Bitte hinterlassen Sie eine Nachricht nach dem Piepton.

- Can I speak to ..., please.
- Can I take a message?
- I've got the wrong number.
- Just a moment, please.
- Who is this, please?
- Please leave a message after the beep.
- This is ...
- I'll phone back later.

b *Sabine Müller is trying to ring her brother, Jan. He is staying with an English family. Complete the dialogues. Use the phrases in* **a**.

MAN Hello?
SABINE Oh, erm ... is that 792 356?
MAN No, it isn't.
SABINE Oh, sorry. I've got the wrong number

ANSWER-PHONE This is 792 356. We can't answer the phone at the moment. Please leave a message after the beep. Thanks.
SABINE Oh nein, es ist der Anrufbeantworter!

WOMAN Hello?
SABINE Hello. This is Sabine. Can I speak to Jan, please
I'm Jan's sister. ____________
WOMAN I'm sorry, Jan's out. Can I take a message?
SABINE It's OK, thanks. I'll phone back later.

Later ...

WOMAN Hello?
SABINE Hello. Is Jan there, please?
WOMAN Who is this, please?
SABINE Oh sorry. It's Sabine, Jan's sister.
WOMAN Oh, of course. Just a moment please.
I'll get him.

p. 10/A1

3 BLUE BOX British and American English → blue box, p. 124

a *Conchita wrote these sentences, so they are in American English (AE). The spelling of one word in each sentence is different in British English (BE). Underline that word. Then write it again with BE spelling.*

> **tip** If you need help with the 'blue box' exercises, look at the vocabulary at the back of your pupil's book.

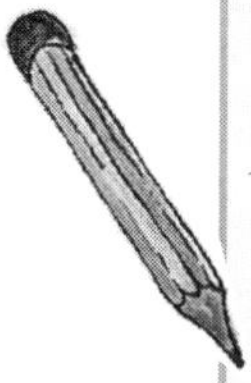

	AE	BE
1	I never go to the theater.	*theatre*
2	Who is your favorite singer?	favourite
3	Pink is a nice color.	colour
4	Do you say 'miles' or 'kilometers'?	kilometres
5	How far is it to the center of the city?	centre
6	I traveled by plane.	travelled
7	I'd love to see New York harbor.	harbour

b *Sometimes Conchita uses words that are different in British English. What is Margo thinking?*

	Conchita	Margo
1	I think Scott is **neat.**	She means *great.*
2	I need an **eraser.**	She means a rubber.
3	**Potato chips** are OK.	She means crisps.
4	But I like **French fries** better.	She means chips.
5	We have to look at the **schedule.**	She means the timetable.
6	It's on the **bulletin board.**	She means the notice board.
7	We have read pages **10 through 20.**	She means pages 10 to 20.
8	My **pants** are dirty.	She means her trousers.
9	Where's the **elevator?**	She means the lift.
10	Careful! There's **garbage on the sidewalk.**	She means the rubbish on the pavement.

p. 10/A2

4 REVISION Yesterday at Space Camp

Put the verbs in the simple past.

Yesterday I (wake up) woke up at 7 o'clock, but I (not, get up) didn't get up until 7.30. I (have) had breakfast in the Milky Way[1] café with the other kids in my team. The food (be) was OK, but I (not, like) didn't like the bread. Josh and I (be) were a bit late for training. The counsellor (not, be) wasn't pleased! In the afternoon we (build) built a great rocket. Well, it (look) looked great, but it (not, fly) didn't fly very well! The others (watch) watched a film in the evening, but I (go) went to bed early and (write) wrote a letter to my family. It (be) was a good day.

[1] Milky Way *Milchstraße*

▶▶▶ NOW YOU

In your exercise book write your diary for one day last week.

5 REVISION Before Space Camp

a *Match the sentence halves.*

1 After Conchita had seen a TV programme about Space Camp
2 Conchita talked to her parents
3 Conchita's parents were really interested
4 After Conchita had read about Space Camp scholarships
5 When Conchita had written her letter to Space Camp
6 Conchita was a bit nervous before her trip to Florida

- when she had found some more information about Space Camp on the Internet.
- because they had always wanted her to travel.
- she asked her teacher for more information about it.
- because she had never travelled alone before.
- she decided to write a letter.
- she waited nervously for the answer.

b *Complete the sentences with the* simple past *or the* past perfect.

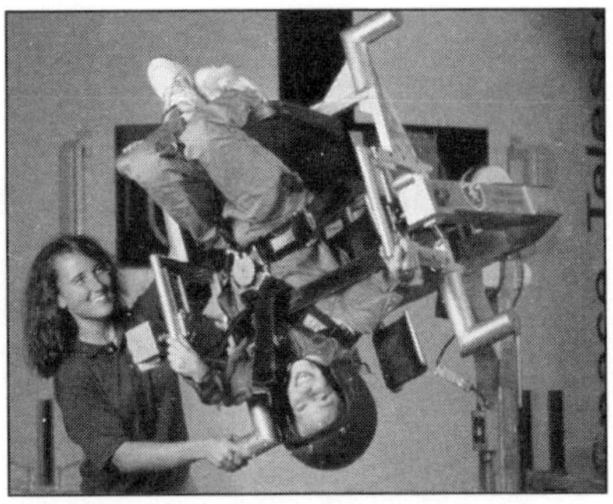

1 After we (eat) had eaten breakfast, we (go) went to the space walk simulator.

2 Joshua (be) was late because he (forgot) had forgotten his helmet.

3 I (be) was really scared because I (never, see) had never seen a simulator before.

4 I (not, get) didn't get into the simulator until the counsellor (explain) had explained everything.

5 When I (finish) had finish, everybody (cheer) cheered.

6 ▶ Pick it up!

Look at the pictures. What are the people saying?
Write a sentence for each picture.
The ideas in the box can help you.

cut • throw pick • put turn • write wake	it the dog the number	away down off on out up

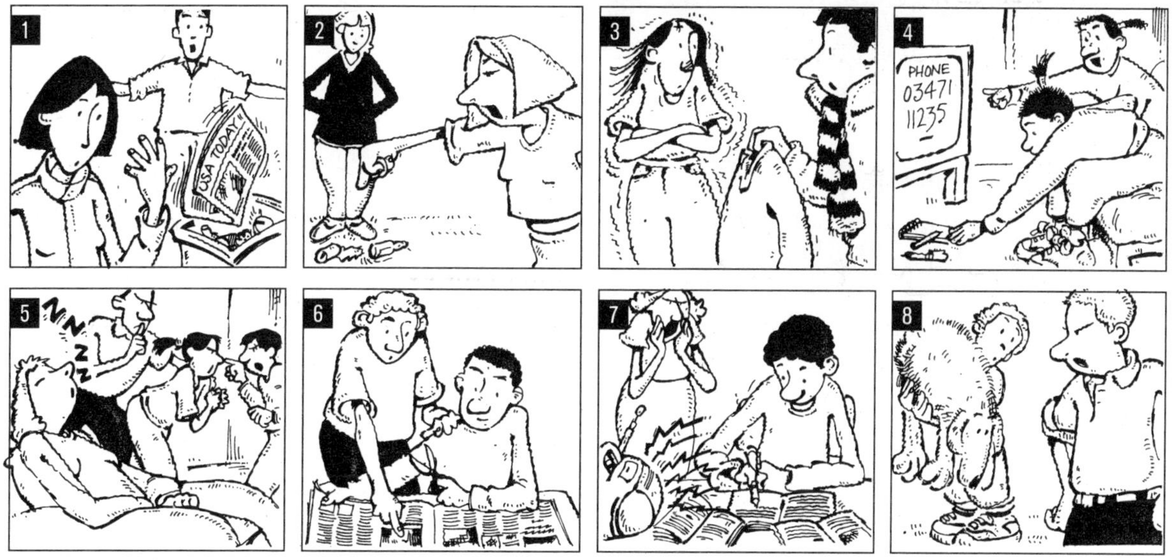

1 *Don't throw it away!*
2 Pick it up!
3 Put it on!
4 Write number down
5 Don't wake her up!
6 Cut it out!
7 Turn it down!
8 Put the dog away !

p. 11/A6

7 ▶ Give it to him!

Complete the sentences. Use pronouns *(*it, him, them, …*) and* to *or* for.

	Personenobjekt	Sachobjekt
Give	me	the money.

	Sachobjekt	Personenobjekt
Give	it	to him.

1 Nancy, show me that photo! – But I showed *it to you* last night.
2 Joshua, teach the others that song. – But I taught it to them last night.
3 Conchita, did you show Glen your diary? – No, I didn't show it to him .
4 Scott, you should send your parents that card. – But I sent it to them yesterday.
5 Conchita, did you send your sister that card? – Yes, I sent it to her yesterday.
6 Conchita's brother wanted a T-shirt. – She got it to him before she left.
7 Mrs Gonzales wanted to cook Conchita a lovely meal for dinner. – She cooked it to her yesterday.
8 Conchita bought her parents a present. – She gave it to them after dinner.

p. 12/A7

8 ▶ A postcard to a friend

Read the postcard on the right. Then imagine you are on holiday. Choose one of the other postcards and write it to a friend.
Write
... where you are,
... what you're doing there,
... what the weather's like,
... what you're going to do the next day.

Dear Jane,
Hi from the USA! I'm having a super time. This place is great. The course is a bit hard. But it's fun — much better than school. The weather is fine every day. I'm leaving tomorrow. My parents and I are going on a trip round Florida before we come home. Say hi to your mum.
Love Margo
PS: Don't forget to send me a postcard.

To
Jane Harr...
43, Sulliv...
London SE...
England

Dear Amy,
Hi from Florida! This is a really great country. I lie on the beach every day. The weather is sunny. Tomorrow I want to go to seaworld because I love dolphins.
I also want to visit the Everglades
Love Ela
PS: I will be back on next Friday!

p. 12/A7

9 ▶ At the fast food kiosk

Complete the conversation. (Tip: Look at the green box on page 86 of your pupil's book for help.)

TOURIST Oh dear, I can't manage this menu.
YOU Can I help?
MAN Frag ihn, was er haben will.
YOU What would you like?
TOURIST I'd like something spicy.
YOU Der Tourist sagt, dass er etwas starkgewürztes möchte.
MAN Wie wäre es mit einer Currywurst?
YOU How about a Currywurst?
TOURIST What's a 'Currywurst'?
YOU A sausage with spicy curry sauce
TOURIST Fine. I'll have one of those and I'd like some chips too, please.
YOU Er möchte eine und Pommes Frites dazu.
MAN Alles klar. Das macht € 2,50.
YOU That costs 2,50€.
TOURIST Great. Thanks very much for your help.

p. 13/A9

WORKING WITH THE TEXT

10 ▶ What happens in the story?

Finish these sentences and retell the story on pages 18–19. Be careful! Only put in important details.

After the trip to Space Camp, Conchita *wants to talk* about her week at Space Camp.

When Conchita goes back to school, her classmates are jealous of her.

Her teacher says the other kids are jealous because they could'nt be at Space Camp.

When Conchita gives her talk about Space Camp, three of her class mates laughed at her and found her talk boring.

But most people in the class want to hear her talk.

At the end of the story Rita says 'it was interesting'.

11 ▶ Everybody's talking

a *After the Science class, everybody is talking about Conchita. Who might say these things?*

1 Hey Rita, Conchita thinks she's so special. She thinks: 'I'm so great, and you guys are so ordinary.' You called her little Miss Astronaut too. And her talk was so boring. Why are you friends with her again? José is angry with you!

2 I think it's really great that Conchita won that scholarship to Space Camp. It was hard for her because some of the other kids in the class were horrible to her. She was sad at first, but I think she has learned something very important.

Person 1 might be Linda. Person 2 might be Ms Morrison.

b *Imagine you are Rita. Write an answer to person 1.*

p. 18–20

1

Unit 1 NOW YOU CAN ...

12 ▶ ... talk with kids at school in English

How do you say these things in English?

1 Was hast du denn?
What's the metter?

2 Halte durch!
Hang in there!

3 Halt den Mund und hör zu!
Shut up and listen!

4 Ich frage mich, was er will.
I wonder, what he wants!

5 Bis morgen.
See you torrow!

13 ▶ ... do this crossword

1 a The American word for 'autumn' — FALL
b A very big room — HALL

2 a You go here to get a plane. — AIRPORT
b When you really want something — DESIRE

3 a 'My train arrives at 6 pm.' – 'OK. I'll come and ... you.' — MEET
b The list of things you can eat in a restaurant — MENU

4 a You do this when you are tired. — YAWN
b An AE word for 'great' or 'fantastic' — AWESOME

14 ▶ ... write about someone you met

Think of an interesting person that you met somewhere. Perhaps you were on holiday, on a school trip, at a party, etc. These questions can help you:

- Where did you meet this person?
- What did you like about him/her?
- What did you do together?
- Did you see him/her again after that?
- Did you write/phone?
- Why/Why not?

I met this person on a birthday party.
He had a very nice outfit.
I played „Blind Cow" with him.
No, I didn't.
Yes, half a year ago.

Unit 1 How to take notes

1 ▶ The main points

a *In this text on the Everglades, you can find information about all the points that are listed in the box. Read the text and underline the important information.*

animals • weather
size • what it is
what grows there
what you can do
where it is

The area of marsh and water in the south of Florida is called the **EVERGLADES**. It's about 110 miles long and its size is 5000 square miles. The water isn't very deep – less than two metres. Lots of trees and long grass grow here.
There are lots of exciting activities to do, for example hiking, canoeing and looking at the wild animals. Tourists really like to see the alligators, but lots of other animals live here, too, like black bears, manatees, and so on.
The weather in the Everglades is very special. The summers are quite long, very hot and rainy. The winters are short and never cold. But there are often hurricanes.

bear [beə] *Bär* manatee [ˌmænəˈtiː]
canoeing [kəˈnuːɪŋ] *Paddeln*
grass [grɑːs] hiking [ˈhaɪkɪŋ] *Wandern*
marsh [mɑːʃ] *Sumpf*

b *Complete these notes. Put in the missing information from the box and the text.*

Manatees

What it is: area of marsh + water (< 2m deep)
Everglades: in s. Florida
Size: 110 mls long / 5000 sq mls
What grows there: lots of trees and long grass
Animals: alligators, black bears, manatee and so on
Activities: e.g. hiking/canoeing/looking at animals
weather: summer – long, v. hot, rainy; winter – short, not cold; often hurricanes.

2 ▶ Short forms and symbols

Look at the text and the notes. Find the meaning of these short forms and symbols.

s.	south	m	metre	v.	very
+	and	e.g.	for example	/	separating Sign
sq mls	Square miles	etc.	and so on	<	smaller than

3 ▶ Take your own notes

a *Underline the words that carry the important information in this text.*

There are often **HURRICANES** in Florida and the south-west of the United States of America. They are very strong winds that move in a circle and bring lots of rain. They usually start over the sea. Winds often reach 120 miles an hour. The funny thing is that in the centre of the hurricane there is no wind, but the sea is very wild. When the hurricanes reach the coast, they cause a lot of damage: for example, they destroy buildings, roads, cars and so on. People often die, too. In 1992, for example, 'Hurricane Andrew' killed 50 people in Florida. Today we can get ready for hurricanes with the help of satellites or planes that check how fast the wind is. This helps to save lives.

circle [ˈsɜːkl] *Kreis* damage [ˈdæmɪdʒ] *Schaden* satellite [ˈsætəlaɪt]

b *Write some notes in your exercise book. Use short forms and symbols where you can.*

Fitness check

How fit are you in English? Do these exercises and check.

1 ▶ Letters to Lizzy

a *Complete Zoe's letter to Lizzy. Use the* simple present.

tip You use the *simple present* when you talk about things that **sometimes, often** or **never** happen, e.g. *He always gets up late at the weekend.*

Dear Lizzy,

We (come) come to Florida every year. We always (stay) stay at the Hotel Playa. It's great in Florida because the sun (shine) shines every day. We (not, go) don't go to the beach at midday – it's too hot for my brother, Zak. He (not, like) doesn't like the sun. He (spend) spends a lot of time in his room. I (love) love it!

Love, Zoe

b *Complete Zak's letter. Use the* present progressive.

tip You use the *present progressive* when something is happening **now**. e.g. *Listen! The baby is crying.*

Dear Lizzy,

I (feel) *'m feeling* fed up. We (spend) are spending our holiday in Florida and it's too hot. The sun (shine) is shining now, so I (not, sit) 'm not sitting outside. I (write) 'm writing this letter in my room. My sister (sit) is sitting by the pool and my dad (swim) is swimming. They (enjoy) are enjoying this holiday. I'm not!

Love, Zak

2 ▶ If you ever go to the Everglades ...

Some of Zoe's friends are going to Florida. Zoe is giving them some information. Write down the sentences in the correct order.

1 – you – go to – the Everglades – you – see – a lot of alligators.
2 – you – only have – a week in Florida – you – not have – time to see everything.
3 – you – listen to – people in the streets – you – hear – English and Spanish.
4 – you – visit – Seaquarium – you – learn – a lot – about – dolphins.
5 – you – eat at – Hispanic restaurant – you – get – wonderful food.
6 – an alligator – catches you – you – not – have – a chance.

1 *If you go to the Everglades, you'll* see a lot of alligators.
2 If you'll have only a week in Florida, you'll haven't time to see everything
3 If you listen to the people in the streets you'll hear English and Spanish.
4 If you visit the Seaquarium, you'll learn a lot about the dolphins
5 If you eat at a Hispanic restaurant, you'll get wonderfull food.
6 If an alligator catches you, you'll don't have a chance.

3 ▶ A perfect crossword

a *Read the clues and complete the crossword with the* past participle.

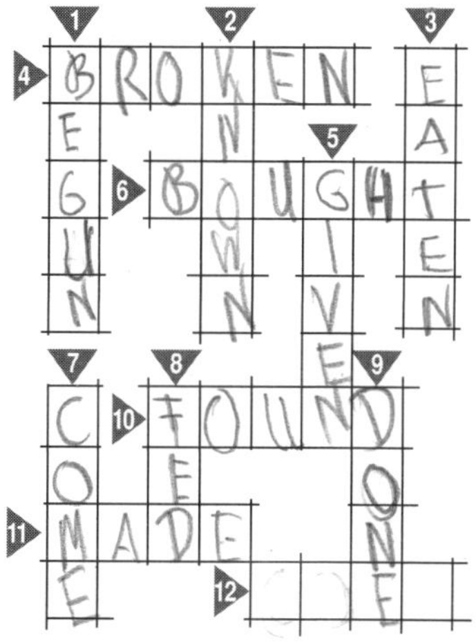

1 The new term has ... . The holidays have finished.
2 How long have you ... your best friend? – I met her two years ago.
3 The dog hasn't ... her food. She must be ill.
4 I can't play football – I've ... my leg.
5 The teacher has ... us a lot of homework. I'm going to start it now.
6 Have you ... a new CD? Can I listen to it?
7 Dad hasn't ... home yet.
8 Have you ... the cat? It looks hungry.
9 Have you ... your homework yet?
10 The Smiths lost their cat last week and they haven't ... it yet.
11 Have you ever ... bread? It's easy to make.
12 Mum has ... home and now she's gone again.

b *Make a table like this in your exercise book. Write down all three forms of the verbs in the crossword.*

Infinitive	Simple past	Past participle
break	*broke*	*broken*
buy	...	...

2 Alaska – the Great Land

1 **BLUE BOX** What do you like better? → blue box, p. 126
Zoe and her new boyfriend Dave are very different! Complete the dialogues with the phrases in the box.

I like to • I'd like to I'd prefer to • Do you want to …? What do you like better …? What do you want to do …?

1 Z What do you like to do at the weekend?
D I like to sleep late and be lazy.
Z Really? I prefer to do sport and keep fit.

2 Z What do you like better – football or basketball?
D I don't like sport.

3 Z What do you want to do today?
D I'd like to do nothing all day.
Z Boring! Do you want to come shopping with me?
D Not really.

4 Z What do you want to do this evening – go to a party or go swimming?
D *I'd prefer to stay at home and watch TV.

p. 24/A1

2 **REVISION** What were they doing?
The teacher was late for the lesson. What were the pupils doing when he arrived? Put the verbs in the correct form.

Tony (bring) *was bringing* some books from the library. Lizzy (film) was filming the others. Zoe (make) was making a model. Susie and Zak (make) were making posters. Harry and Will (not, work) weren't working. They (fight) were fighting. Bert and Dave (not, help) weren't helping the others. Bert (listen) was listening to music and Dave (sleep) was sleeping!

*Word

3 REVISION What jobs has Glen finished?

Look at Glen's list.
What jobs has he done and what hasn't he done yet?

TO DO:
finish homework ✓
have dinner ✓
read book about Epcot ✓
write report on Space Camp ✗
buy dad a birthday present ✗
send Margo a postcard ✓
call Conchita ✗

1 He has finished homework.
2 He has had dinner.
3 He has read a book about Epcot.
4 He hasn't written the report on Space Camp
5 He hasn't bought dad a birthday present
6 He has sent Margo a postcard
7 He hasn't called Conchita.

4 ▶ How long have they been at this school?

Put in for *or* since.

▶▶▶ NOW YOU

Write four sentences like this:

I	have haven't	known seen been lived	my girlfriend/boyfriend/my grandparents in the swimming/basketball/… club in this town/school/class … in our flat …	for … since …

1 I haven't known my girlfriend for two years.
2 I have been in the swimming since three years.
3 I haven't lived in this school for a half year.
4 I have seen my boyfriend for years ago.

p. 24/A3

5 REVISION Simple past or present perfect?

Complete the dialogue.

BOY How long (you, be) ____________________ here?

GIRL I (not, be) __________________ here long.

BOY What time (you, arrive) ____________________ ?

GIRL I (get) _____ here at six o'clock.

BOY (you, already buy) ______________________________ __________ the tickets?

GIRL No, because I (not, have) ________________ enough money.

BOY (you, be) ____________________ here before?

GIRL I (be) ___________ here last week and (see) ___________ a Star Wars film.

BOY I (see) ___________ that film two weeks ago. It (be) ___________ great, wasn't it?

tip Be careful. The German *Perfekt* can be present perfect or simple past.

e.g. *Ich habe ein Buch gekauft.* = **I've bought** a book.
You often use the present perfect with words like: **just, already, never, before, not ... yet, since, for**

But *Ich habe gestern ein Buch gekauft.* = **I bought** a book yesterday.
You often use the simple past with time expressions like: **yesterday, two days ago, last week ...**

6 ▶ How long have you been doing it?

Complete the sentences with for *or* since.

1 I've been doing my piano practice ________ an hour and I still can't play this song!

2 How long have you been collecting bottles? – ________ 1964.

3 How long has she been watching TV? – ________ four o'clock.

4 How long have they been running ? – ________ about half an hour.

5 Stop now. You've been sitting at that computer ________ breakfast.

6 She has been building that castle ________ ten o'clock this morning.

7 People have been swimming here ________ ages.

p. 25/A5

7 ▶ A talk about whaling

Imagine your Science teacher has asked you and a partner to give a talk on whaling. You have found some information on the Internet – but it's in English. Complete the conversation. (Tip: look at page 86 of your pupil's book for help.)

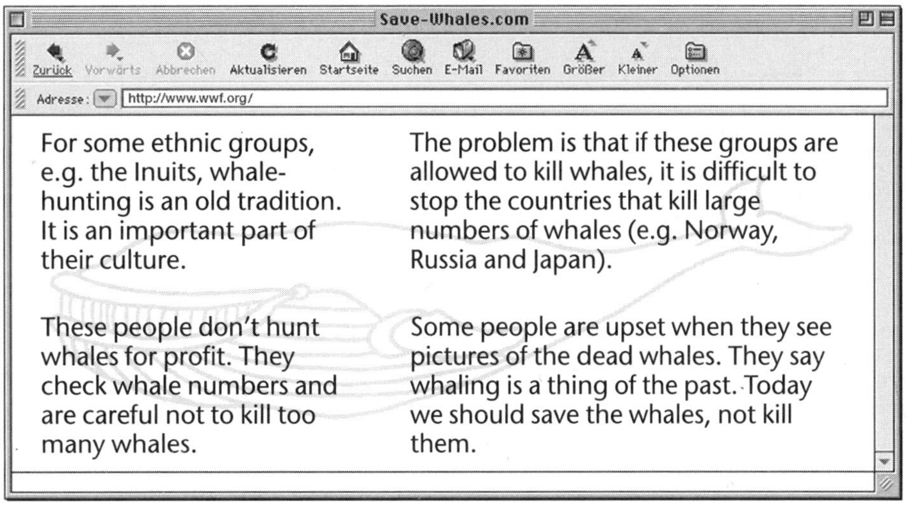

PARTNER Wir brauchen einige Punkte für den Walfang.

YOU Also hier steht, dass für ein paar ethnische Gruppen, wie die Inuits, der Walfang eine alte Tradition ist. Er ist ein bedeutender Teil ihrer Kultur.

PARTNER Prima. Gibt es noch etwas?

YOU Hier steht noch, dass diese Leute die Wale nicht für Geld jagen. Sie überprüfen die Walpopulation und töten nicht zu viele.

PARTNER Gut. Jetzt brauchen wir einige Punkte gegen den Walfang.

YOU Das Problem ist, wenn man diesen Gruppen das Töten von Walen erlaubt, ist es schwierig die Länder, die grosse Anzahlen an Walen töten (z.B. Norwegen, Russland und Japan) zu stoppen.

PARTNER Toll. Findest du noch einen Punkt?

YOU Einige Leute sind aufgebracht, wenn sie Bilder mit toten Walen sehen. Sie sagen, Walfang ist Vergangenheit. Heute sollten wir die Wale schützen, nicht töten.

p. 25/A5

8 ▶ REVISION Which words can go together?

Tick the right boxes.

	building	feeling	film	mistake	man	party	population
big	✓			✓		✓	
large							✓
tall					✓		
great		✓	✓			✓	

▶▶▶ NOW YOU

Complete the sentences for yourself.

Raumschiff Surprise is the greatest film I've seen.

Ralf is the tallest person I know.

Bodensee is the largest lake I know.

Stuttgart is the biggest city I've been to.

9 ▶ Amy's dream holiday

Sometimes Amy thinks about her dream holiday.
Complete the sentences. Use the correct forms of the verbs.

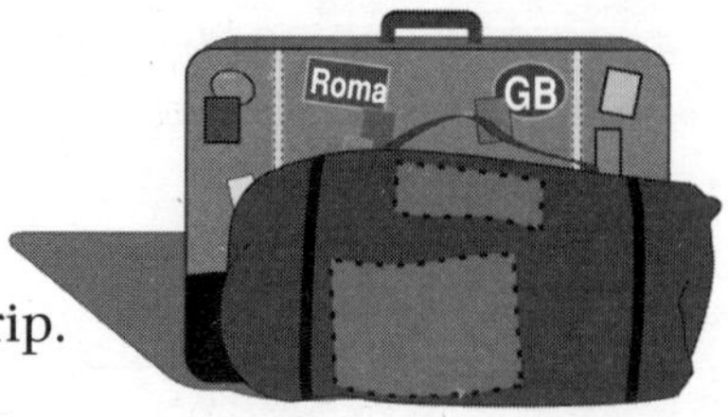

1 If I (have) *had* lots of money, I would go on my dream trip.

2 If I (travel) travelled alone, I might be lonely.

3 If I could go wherever I wanted, I (choose) chose Europe.

4 If my best friend wanted to come, I (take) would take her with me.

5 If she (not, want) wouldn't wan to come, I (ask) would ask dad.

6 If I (go) went to England, I (not, have) wouldn't have a problem with the language.

7 If I (visit) visited Germany, I (not, understand) wouldn't understand the local people.

8 My grandma (be) was sad if I (not, send) wouldn't send her a postcard from every place I visited.

▶▶▶ NOW YOU

Finish these sentences. Use your own ideas. If you need help, you can use the ideas below.

1 If we didn't have cars, there wouldn't be so many accidents.

2 If there were no computers, there would be no computer games and e-mail.

3 My life would be perfect if I win the Lotto.

4 If I lived in Alaska, I would hate the long winters and like the long days in summer.

5 I'd get really angry if someone took my bike.

p. 27/A8

10 SOUNDS Stressed syllables

Say these words. Where's the stress?
Put them into the correct list.

alligator • American • astronaut
combine • concentrate • culture
embarrass • explore • important
interested • Japan • nervous • programme
project • religion • season • student
tomorrow • tradition • vacation

Stress on the first syllable as in 'whaling'		Stress on the second syllable as in 'adventure'	
alligator	nervous	American	Japan
astronaut	programme	combine	student
concentrate	project	embarrass	tomorrow
culture	religion	explore	tradition
interested	season	important	vacation

p. 27/A8

11 ▶ Plurals

Write down the plurals of these words.
One word in each group has a different kind of plural. (Circle) it.

wolf	wolves	mouse	mouses	photo	photos	fish	fish
family	families	foot	(feet)	life	lives	city	cities
thief	thieves	animal	animals	guy	guys	enemy	enemies
knife	knives	tooth	tooths	valley	valleys	story	stories

p. 28/A9

12 ▶ A sad story

Complete the text with the correct form of the verbs in the box.

attack • avoid • call • cut
fight • make fun • protect

There's a horrible gang of kids at school. They ______________ me names and ______________ of me. They wait for me after school. I try to go home a different way and ______________ them, but I can't escape from them. Yesterday they all ______________ me. They jumped on me, and hit me. I ______________ back, but there were too many of them. They took my English book and ______________ it up into little pieces. My big brother is very strong. He says he'll ______________ me, but he can't always be with me.

p. 28/A10

WORKING WITH THE TEXT

13 ▶ Camping and hunting

Complete the network with words from the text on pages 33–35. Add more lines and words if you can.

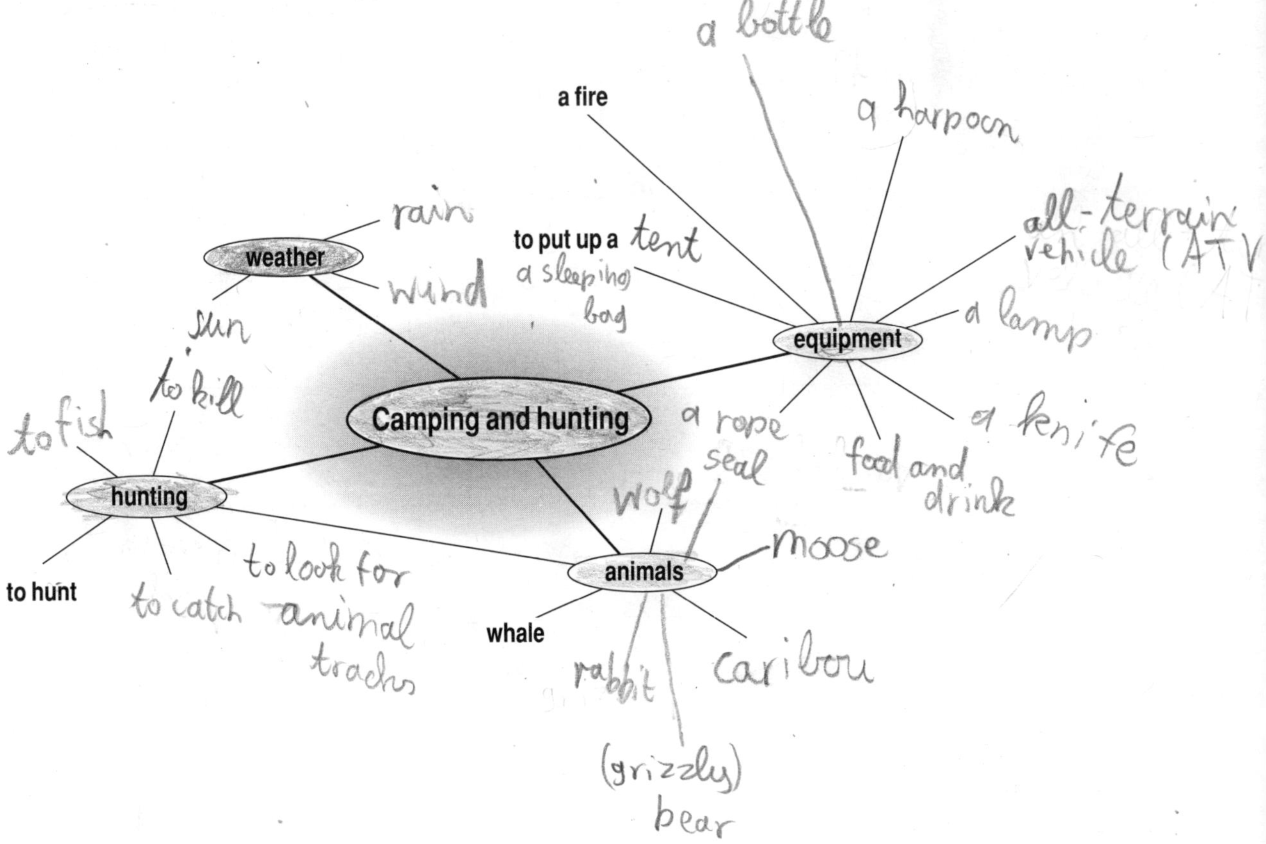

14 ▶ An interview with Lester Swenson

Imagine Lester is back in Barrow. How might he answer these questions?

Q Mr Swenson, you have just got back after an exciting adventure. How did you feel when you woke up and your friend had left?

A *At first* I was shocked. I worried about my friend. I was frightened
But then I thought about I could survive. I had to make a fire to get warm and I had to look for water and food.

Q And was it difficult to survive?

A *At first* I thought I would soon a dead man.
But then I remembered how the early Inuits had made fires. I hit together two stones to get sparks. In mine environ[ment] I had found wood. With a fire knife I cut a round piece of nylon out of my tent. And made a bottle. I put snow on it and hang it near of

x I looked for animal tracks in the snow and I caught a rabbit with my hands.

Q What would you say to your friend if you met him now?

A *If I met Henry,* I would tell him that I understand him now. I know that he was trying to teach me a lesson.

Q One last question, Mr Swenson. Would you like to go camping again soon?

A Not in the next time. And when I will go camping again I will take some equipment with me.

pp. 33–35

15 ▶ ... be miserable in English

How do you say these things in English?

1 Ich habe einen harten Tag gehabt.
I have had a hard day.

2 Ich habe seit dem Frühstück nichts gegessen.
I haven't eaten anything since breakfast.

3 Ich habe mir den Finger verbrannt.
I have burned me the finger.

4 Ich bin erkältet.
I have a cold.

5 Ich friere!
I feel cold! I'm freezing!

16 ▶ ... find the group words

What are they?

1 Dinner is a *meal*.
2 Summer is a season.
3 A car is a vehicle.
4 The Inuits are native people.
5 A wolf is a(n) animal.
6 The USA is a (big) country.
7 Alaska is a state.
8 Anchorage is a town.
9 The Mississippi is a river.
10 Denali is a mountain and a National Park.

17 ▶ ... write about the trip you'd like to make

Where would you like to go? The USA? Alaska perhaps? Or Florida? Or would you prefer somewhere different? Write about your dream trip. The questions in the box can help you.

Where would you go? Why?	What/Who would you take photos of?
Who would you take with you? Why?	Who would you like to meet there?
What would/wouldn't you do?	Would you take home any souvenirs?
What would you like to see and where?	

I would like to go to the state of Florida, because there is so much to see and it's always sunny there. I would take my whole family with me, because it's better to travel in a group and it makes more fun. I would like to see some tourist attractions. I would like to see the Kennedy Space Center and I would like to make a visit to the theme park „Seaworld" in Orlando, because I'm a dolphin lover. I would like to take a photo of a real rocket, of dolphins, and of some fish. In the Space Camp I would like to meet a real astronaut. I would as souvenirs a brochure of the Space Camp and some postcards

Unit 2 How to use a dictionary (German-English)

1 ▶ Getting to know your dictionary

a *Find the* running heads *on this page and* (circle) *them.*

b *Look at the* running heads *only. Don't look at the rest of the page.*
Do you think you'll find the words below on this page?

	yes	no
Hektar	X	
Hektik	X	
heftig		X
heraus		X
herab	X	

Look for the words on the page to check your answers.

c *Find words with* **two** *translations and circle them.*

d *Find a word with* **three** *translations and draw a* box *around it.*

e *Find a word with* **more than three** *translations.* Underline *it.*

heiraten 473 **heranwachsend**

heiraten get* married /get 'mærid/, marry* /'mæri/ **Sie werden im Juni heiraten.** They're getting married in June.

Get married ist gebräuchlicher als **marry: When are Sue and Ian getting married?** Wann heiraten Sue und Ian? **Are you getting married in church?** Heiratet ihr kirchlich? **They got married in 1992.** Sie haben 1992 geheiratet.

Heiratsantrag proposal /prə'pəʊzl/ **(jdm) einen Heiratsantrag machen** propose /prə'pəʊz/ (to sb)

heiser hoarse /hɔ:s/ (*Adv* hoarsely) **Er ist ganz heiser.** He's lost his voice.

heiß 1 hot* /hɒt/ **Die Teller sind heiß.** The plates are hot. **Heute ist es heiß.** It's hot today. **Mir ist heiß.** I'm hot.
2 (*Diskussion, Auseinandersetzung*) heated /'hi:tɪd/; (*Thema*) controversial /ˌkɒntrə'vɜ:ʃl/ **Das Gebiet ist heiß umkämpft.** The area is fiercely fought over.

heißen 1 be* called /kɔ:ld/ **Wie heißt Ihre Frau?** What's your wife called? **Ich heiße Walter.** My name is Walter.
2 mean* /mi:n/ (*nicht in ing-Formen*) **Was heißt „Tür" auf englisch?** What is the English for 'Tür'? **„Tür" heißt auf englisch „door".** The English for 'Tür' is 'door'. **Was soll das heißen?** What do you mean by that?
◆ **das heißt** that is to say … **es heißt, dass** … they say that … **jdn willkommen heißen** welcome /'welkəm/ sb

heiter (*Mensch*) cheerful /'tʃɪəfl/ (*Adv* cheerfully /'tʃɪəfəli/) (*Wetter*) fair /feə(r)/; (*Buch, Artikel*) light-hearted /ˌlaɪt 'hɑ:tɪd/
◆ **aus heiterem Himmel ⇨ Himmel**

heizen heat /hi:t/ **mit Strom heizen** use electricity for heating **Der Ofen heizt gut.** The heater is very efficient.

Heiz- Heizgerät heater /'hi:tə(r)/ **Heizkörper** radiator /'reɪdieɪtə(r)/

Heizung heating /'hi:tɪŋ/; (*Heizkörper*) radiator /'reɪdieɪtə(r)/ **eine Heizung einbauen** put in central heating

Hektar hectare /'hekteə(r)/ (*Abkürz* ha)

Hektik hectic rush **die Hektik des modernen Lebens** the hectic pace of modern life **die Hektik der Großstadt** the hectic life of the city

hektisch hectic /'hektɪk/ (*Adv* hectically /'hektɪkli/) frantic /'fræntɪk/ (*Adv* frantically /'fræntɪkli/) **eine hektische Suche** a frantic search

Held hero* /'hɪərəʊ/

heldenhaft heroic /hɪ'rəʊɪk/ (*Adv* heroically /hɪ'rəʊɪkli/)

Heldin heroine /'herəʊɪn/

helfen help /help/ **Könntest du mir beim Kochen helfen?** Could you help me with the cooking? **Ich half ihr, die Party zu organisieren.** I helped her to organize the party. **jdm über die Straße helfen** help sb across the road
◆ **es hilft nichts** it's no good **ich kann mir nicht helfen** I can't help it **Ich kann mir nicht helfen, aber ich mag ihn nicht.** I can't help not liking him. **jdm aus der Patsche helfen ⇨ Patsche; jdm ist nicht mehr zu helfen** sb is a hopeless case

Helfer(in) helper /'helpə(r)/

hell 1 light /laɪt/ **Im Sommer ist es früh hell.** In summer it's light early. **ein heller Raum** a light room
2 (*Licht, Lampe*) bright /braɪt/ (*Adv* brightly) **ein hell leuchtender Stern** a brightly shining star
3 (*Kleidung, Holz etc*) light-coloured /ˌlaɪt 'kʌləd/ (*AE* light-colored) **eine helle Hose** light-coloured trousers
4 (*Haut, Haare*) fair /feə(r)/
5 helles Bier lager /'lɑ:gə(r)/

hell- hellblau light blue **hellblond** very fair

Helligkeit brightness /'braɪtnəs/

hellsehen hellsehen können be* able to see into the future

hellwach wide awake /ˌwaɪd ə'weɪk/

Helm helmet /'helmɪt/

Hemd shirt /ʃɜ:t/

Hemisphäre hemisphere /'hemɪsfɪə(r)/

Hemmung inhibition /ˌɪnhɪ'bɪʃn/

hemmungslos without restraint /wɪˌðaʊt rɪ'streɪnt/

Henkel handle /'hændl/

Henne hen /hen/

her 1 etwas ist … her sth is* … ago /ə'gəʊ/ **Wie lange ist das jetzt her?** How long ago is it now? **Es ist vier Jahre her, dass wir uns das letzte Mal gesehen haben.** It's four years since we last saw each other.
2 hinter jdm/etwas her sein be* after sb/sth **Die Polizei ist schon lange hinter dem Verbrecher her.** The police have been after the criminal for a long time. **Sie ist nur hinter seinem Geld her.** She's only after his money.
3 von … her sein be* from … **Wo bist denn du her? Aus Köln?** Where are you from? Cologne?
◆ **her damit!** give me that! **Her mit dem Geld!** Hand over your money! **hin und her ⇨ hin; von … her ⇨ von**

herab down /daʊn/

herab- ☛ Siehe auch **hinab-, hinunter-, herunter-.**

herabsetzen 1 (*Standard*) lower /'ləʊə(r)/; (*Preis, Steuern, Geschwindigkeit*) reduce /rɪ'dju:s; *AE* rɪ'du:s/
2 (*schlecht machen*) belittle /bɪ'lɪtl/

Herabsetzung reduction /rɪ'dʌkʃn/

herangehen an etwas herangehen go* /gəʊ/ up to sth; (*an ein Problem etc*) approach /ə'prəʊtʃ/ sth

herankommen an jdn/etwas herankommen get* /get/ at sb/sth **Das Auto kam langsam heran.** The car approached slowly. **An das oberste Regal komme ich nicht heran.** I can't reach the top shelf. **Wie bist du an die Platte herangekommen?** How did you get hold of the record?

heranschleichen (sich) (an jdn/etwas) heranschleichen sneak /sni:k/ up (on sb/sth)

herantreten an jdn/etwas herantreten approach /ə'prəʊtʃ/ sb/sth

heranwachsend growing /'grəʊɪŋ/ **ein heranwach-**

en	əʊ	pi:	kju:	ɑ:(r)	es	ti:	ju:	vi:	'dʌblju:	eks	waɪ	zed, zi:
n	o	p	q	r	s	t	u	v	w	x	y	z

2 ▶ Symbols and short forms

Find these short forms and symbols on the dictionary page. Match them to the correct long forms.

⇨	= adverb
jdm	= American English
jdn	= and so on
sb	= irregular form
Adv	= jemandem
AE	= jemanden
sth	= somebody
etc	= something
*	= go to another headword

3 ▶ Dictionary practice

Look up the German words and correct the mistakes.

1 We had a ~~hot~~ conversation. I got very angry.
heiß = heated

2 The weather was very ~~cheerful~~ yesterday.
heiter = fair

3 You should ~~put down~~ your prices.
herabsetzen = (to) lower

4 She has got very ~~bright~~ hair. hell = fair

5 I can ~~get~~ the top shelf.
herankommen = (to) reach

p. 36

3 Dreamland California

1 ▶ Things you can do in a National Park

Use verbs to complete the text.

You can do so many things in America's National Parks.

__________ a mountain,

_____ for a walk in a deep canyon,

_______ a horse,

_________ a bridge over a wild river,

_______ photos of giant trees,

__________ a tent in a beautiful camp-site,

_____ for a bike ride along a lovely valley.

Feel tired? __________ a video in a visitor centre!

Whatever you do, you'll _________ a fantastic time. We promise!

p. 42/A4

2 BLUE BOX 50 miles an hour → blue box, p. 131.

Look at the signs. Then complete the sentences with phrases from the box.

$1 a cup • $2 a glass • $10 a bottle • once a week
twice a day • four times a day
six days a week • 50 miles an hour

1 The wine costs ______________________.
2 The speed limit is ______________________.
3 The restaurant is open ______________________.
4 The orange juice costs ______________________.
5 The tea costs ______________________.
6 The adventure club meets ______________________.
7 There's a talk ______________________.
8 There's a video show ______________________.

▶▶▶ NOW YOU

Answer the questions. Use phrases like: once a week, two hours a day, *etc.*

How often do you get homework? ______________________

How often do you do sport? ______________________

How much TV do you watch? ______________________

How much does cola cost in your local café? ______________________

p. 42/A4

3 REVISION Bigger and better

a *Complete the table.*

bad	______	*the* ______
big	______	______
exciting	______	______
famous	______	______
good	______	______
hot	______	______
tall	______	______

b *Complete the text with words from the table.*

In California everything is (big) ______ and (good) ______ than any other place in the world. They have (tall) ______ trees in the world and (big) ______ films. They think that they have (good) ______ software companies in the world and (famous) ______ film stars. They also have (hot) ______ place on Earth and some people think they have (bad) ______ earthquakes too.

Just for fun

Q: Which burn longer – the candles on a boy's birthday cake or the candles on a girl's birthday cake?
A: Don't be silly. Candles burn shorter not longer!

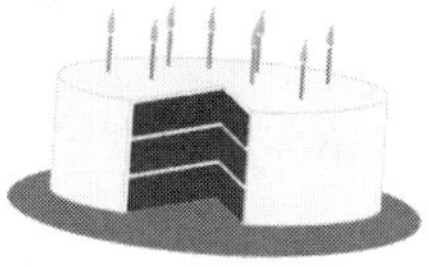

4 REVISION Word building

Make nouns with the ending -ness *from the adjectives in the box and complete the sentences.*

dark • fit • homeless • ill • kind • lonely • nervous

1. ______ is very important for many Americans. People want to look good.
2. In big cities not everyone has a place to live. ______ is a problem.
3. Winter in Alaska – that means more than two months of total ______.
4. Many of the 49ers worked alone. One of their biggest problems was ______.
5. I'm very shy with new people. I'm sure everybody notices my ______.
6. Sorry, I can't come tomorrow. I'm not well. – Oh dear, I hope it's not a serious ______.
7. I really enjoyed my stay with you and your family. Thanks for all your ______.

5 ▶ The Golden Gate Bridge

Complete the crossword.

1 When the 49ers left, Bodie became a ... town.
2 The British say 'film', the Americans say '...'.
3 What's the fourth word? hot – cold warm – ...
4 In 1848 the ... rush started in California.
5 Many black people weren't free – they were ... .
6 Bodie was a gold-... town.
7 The man who designed the Golden Gate Bridge came from ... .
8 The ground is shaking – it's an ... .
9 You mustn't drive faster than 40 miles an hour. There's a ... .
10 What's the ... today? – It's 30 °C.
11 When you cross the Golden Gate Bridge, you only pay when you are travelling ... .
12 A hot, dry area.
13 The place where they make films.
14 This is what you want most of all if you aren't free.
15 You write '25 °C'. You say '25 ... Celsius'.
16 What's the fourth word? live – life die – ...

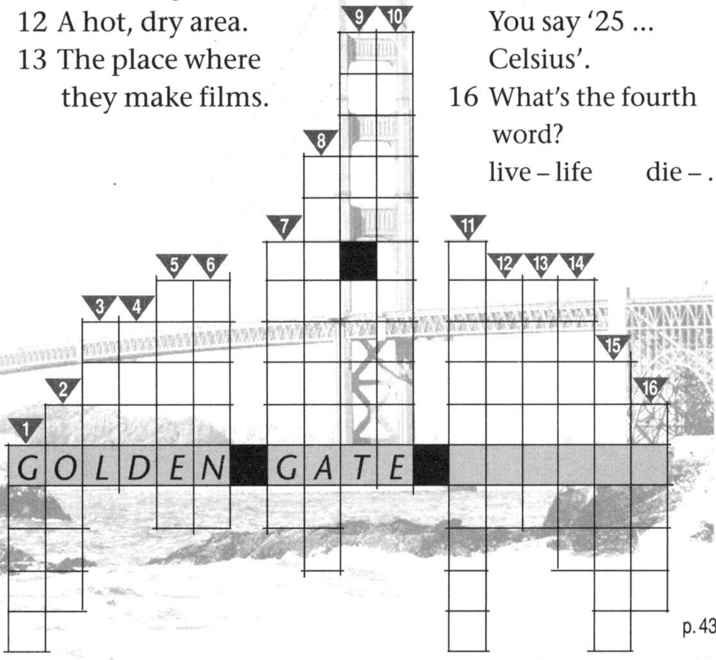

p. 43/A7

6 ▶ Questions, questions

You 'meet' an Italian boy in a chat room. His family has just moved to California. Write these questions to him.

1 When - move to America?

____

2 Why - leave Italy?

____

3 like California?

____

4 What Italian things - miss?

____

5 visit Italy sometimes?

____

6 Have got brothers and sisters?

____

7 speak English or Italian at home?

____

8 go to an American school?

____

▶▶▶ NOW YOU

What else can you ask him? Write five more questions in your exercise book.

p. 43/A7

7 ▶ An interview for a music magazine

These were the singer's answers. What were the reporter's questions?

tip This exercise has subject questions and object questions. Do you remember the difference?

*Willst du wissen, **wer's** gemacht, sind 'do / does / did' nicht angebracht. Willst du wissen, '**Wem?**' oder '**Wen?**', dann müssen 'do / does / did' dort stehn.*

1 Where ________________ when you were a child? — I lived in Haiti until I was seven, then I moved to the US.

2 Who ________________? — My mum taught me to sing. She's a great singer.

3 Where ________________ ________________? — I met all the other people in the band at school. We're old friends.

4 How often ________________? — We practised all the time.

5 Who ________________ ________________? — We all chose the name of the band. Don't you think it's great?

6 Who ________________ ________________? — I listened to Bob Marley a lot when I was a teenager.

7 When ________________ ________________? — Our first CD came out in 1994.

8 When ________________? — We became really famous in 1995 when our second CD came out.

p. 43/A7

8 ▶ Teenage feelings

Use the words in the boxes and complete the poems.

learning • doing • shouting • fighting

Start ____________ your homework!
Stop ____________ with your brother!
Start ____________ your English!
Stop ____________ at your mother!

bad • exciting • happy • sad

Getting letters makes me ____________ .
Hearing bad news makes me ____________ .
Going on holiday is ____________ .
Being angry is ____________ .

like • don't like • hate • love

I ____________ walking in the rain.
I ____________ standing in the cold.
I ____________ sitting in the sun.
I ____________ wearing gold.

▶▶▶ NOW YOU

Write your own poem in your exercise book.

p. 44/A11

9 ▶ All about me

Answer this e-mail. Do you like the things Kelly likes? Tell her about the things you like, and the things you hate. Do you think you could be friends?

All about me – Microsoft Outlook

To... Christian

Cc...

Subject: All about me

Hi!

My name is Kelly Bayford and I'm a student at Kennedy High School, Hollywood, USA. I'm 14 years old and I like sports, e.g. baseball and swimming.
I also like watching Star Trek, eating spicy food, getting up early and going for long walks with my dog.

Going to school is OK. I hate visiting museums and going camping :-(
Do you like the same things? Write and tell me all about yourself!!

Kelly

p. 44/A11

10 ▶ One sentence only

Make one sentence out of two. Use gerunds.

1 I don't want to listen to this song any more. I'm fed up with it.

I'm fed up with ______________________.

2 I go out alone at night. I'm not scared.

I'm not scared of ______________________.

3 My dad gave me a mobile phone. I thanked him.

I thanked my dad for ______________________.

4 I'm going on holiday soon. I'm looking forward to that.

5 I don't follow traditions. I don't believe in it.

6 My parents don't want to move to a different country. They can't imagine it.

7 I'd love to go to New York. I often dream of that.

p. 45/A13

3

11 ▶ SOUNDS

Do they sound the same or different? Tick the correct boxes.

	same	different		same	different
1 movie – cool	☐	☐	6 store – war	☐	☐
2 death – neat	☐	☐	7 fair – year	☐	☐
3 sea – area	☐	☐	8 slave – have	☐	☐
4 weight – celebrate	☐	☐	9 speed – people	☐	☐
5 desert – detail	☐	☐	10 earth – work	☐	☐

p. 45/A13

12 ▶ Explaining traditions

Complete this conversation at the Tet Festival in San Francisco. (Look at the green box on page 86 in your pupil's book for help.)

GERMAN TOURIST Hast du eine Ahnung, worum es hier geht? Warum werden diese ganzen Knallkörper angezündet? Du sprichst doch Englisch. Frag doch mal den Mann da.

YOU Excuse me, ____?

VIETNAMESE AMERICAN We always light them at Tet. They are against evil spirits.

YOU ____

GERMAN TOURIST Frag ihn, was für ein Fest sie gerade feiern.

YOU ____

VIETNAMESE AMERICAN It's the Vietnamese spring festival. It's called Tet.

YOU ____

____

VIETNAMESE AMERICAN You're from Germany, aren't you? What traditions do you have?

YOU Er will wissen, ____.

GERMAN TOURIST Eine gute Frage.

▶▶▶ NOW YOU

Think of a tradition that people in your area follow. How would you explain it to a someone from another country?

____

____

____

____

____

Christmas biscuits

Beer Festival

Carneval

p. 45/A13

WORKING WITH THE TEXT

13 ▶ What does it really mean?

Find these sentences in the text on pages 50–52 of your pupil's book.
What exactly do they mean? Choose from the ideas below.

1 Well, she's not exactly my girlfriend.
 a Rodney would like Ivy to be his girlfriend. ✓
 b Rodney doesn't want Ivy to be his girlfriend.

2 Guys like Lavell Tyler don't breathe the same air as guys like me.
 a Rodney thinks he's better than Lavell.
 b Rodney thinks Lavell is better than him.

3 When she came into class she looked like someone had died.
 a Ivy looked very upset.
 b Ivy told Rodney someone had died.

4 'I felt like a total fool.'
 a Ivy felt a bit silly when she saw Lavell and Deleisha.
 b Ivy felt very silly when she saw Lavell and Deleisha.

5 'I told him what he could do with that idea.'
 a Ivy said it's no problem if Lavell sees Deleisha too.
 b Ivy told Lavell she doesn't want to see him any more.

6 Music, that was what those words were.
 a Rodney heard music.
 b Rodney was very happy.

7 'You stay reliable, you hear what I'm saying, Rodney?'
 a Ivy wants a boyfriend who doesn't go out with other girls.
 b Ivy wants a boyfriend who is cool.

14 ▶ Guess what!

Rodney often writes e-mails to his friends. What do you think he wrote in these messages?

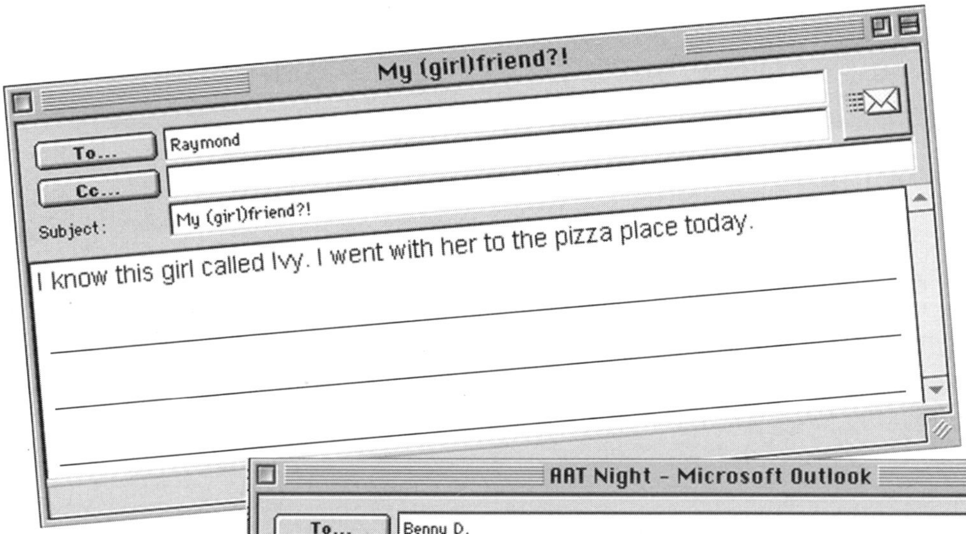

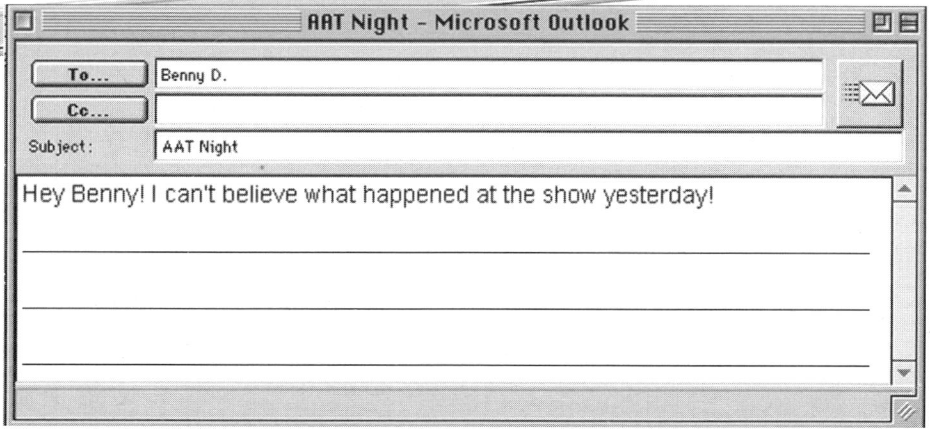

15 ▶ talk about your interests in English

How do you say these things in English?

1 Ich gehe gern ins Kino.

____

____

2 Ich sehe sehr gern Gruselfilme.

____

____

3 Ich spiele gut Klavier.

____

____

4 Es ist interessanter, mich mit Freunden zu treffen als Hausaufgaben zu machen.

____

____

____

5 Ich träume davon, Schauspieler/in zu werden.

____

____

16 ▶ find the odd one out

One word in each group is different. Circle it. Can you add any words to the groups?

piano	cassette	cartoon	actor
reggae	classical	action	writer
cello	pop	rehearsal	director
violin	rock	horror	synthesizer
drums	rap	science fiction	camera person

17 ▶ write for the school newspaper

Have you seen a great film this month? Or heard a great song? Maybe you've seen a play or a concert? Or perhaps there's a great programme on TV that you think other people should watch?
Write a short article like Julie's for the school newspaper.

Last week I went to a talent show. Lots of kids from our school were in it. Everybody was really good, but the best act was Ice Happa (Rodney Suyama and Ivy Ramos). Rodney did a rap and Ivy walked up and down with a drum. The best bit was when they both landed on the floor. It was the funniest thing I have ever seen! You can see them at our school talent show this week. Don't miss it!

Julie Muramoto

____

____

____

____

____

____

____

1 ▶ Getting started

Your job is to write 50–60 words about Los Angeles. You can choose a topic: weather *or* history. *First look at the three texts on this page. The useful information is underlined.*

tip There will be some words on this page that you may not understand. Don't worry. Concentrate on the information that you want. If you really think the word is important, use a dictionary.

From a travel guide

history

Until 1848 California was part of Mexico. It was then sold to the USA. That is why there is so much Spanish spoken there today. In 1848 and 1849 gold was discovered there. Thousands of people went west to California to try to find some. Today it is still called the 'golden state'. In 1850 California became an American state.

The tourist industry is very important here. The area in and around L.A. offers a lot to people who have free time on their hands. Beach-lovers are at home there – they can go swimming, surfing, sailing and windsurfing. Fishing and rock climbing are also popular.

Believe it or not, you can also go skiing near L.A., from December until April.

But if you prefer to watch other people do the work, then go to one of the big baseball games (from April to October) or watch the L.A. Lakers, the famous basketball team.

From a website

Favoriten Verlauf Suchen Seiten

You can go to L.A. at any time during the year – winter or summer. August and September are the hottest months when temperatures can reach 32 °C. January and February are the coolest and wettest months. But winter temperatures are often around 12°C – not very cold. The average[1] temperature is 21°C. If you go to L.A. in the summer the beaches will be very full. If you want to visit one of the National Parks you should book. They are busy too.

[1] average ['ævərɪdʒ] *Durchschnitts-, durchschnittlich*

From a multimedia encyclopedia

weather

Los Angeles is famous for its nice weather, films and TV industry, earthquakes, fires and smog.

history

A group of Spanish people first arrived in 1781. The railway arrived in the 1870s and the city began to grow. By 1900 the population had reached 100,000. In 2000 it was 3.5 million.

Today L.A. is one of the most important centres of industry in the USA. Electronic equipment, clothes, food and chemicals are produced there. The city is also famous for its space industry.

2 ▶ Make notes

a *Complete these notes so that you can write a paragraph on one topic in your exercise book.*

weather	history
nice	1781: ...
hottest time: ...	1848/49: ...
temp.: ...	1850: ...
coolest time: ...	1870s: ...
temp.: ...	1900: ...
av. temp.: ...	2000: ...

b *Write a short paragraph from your notes Try not to look at the texts!*

3 ▶ The next step

Your next job is to write about industry *and* outdoor activities *in L.A.*

a *Read through the three texts on this page. Underline the important points and write* industry *or* outdoor activities *next to them.*

b *Make notes about them.*

c *Write a paragraph on each of the topics.*

p. 53

Revision (Units 1–3)

1 ▶ A trip to a National Park

A class is discussing where they want to go on a trip. What are they saying?

At Frederick Sound in Alaska, you can often see 50 whales at one time.

Highest temperatures in Florida in the summer are about 32 degrees.

In Death Valley, nothing grows. The only animals are rabbits and wild sheep.

Yosemite National Park is full of wonderful animals – you can see bears and 60 other different animals. In Yosemite you can also see giant trees, huge waterfalls, and the second highest mountain in the US – Mount Whitney.

1 go to Alaska / see some whales
If we went to Alaska, we would see some whales.

2 visit Florida / temperatures / be too high for me
If we ________________________________
________________________________ .

3 choose Death Valley / not see any interesting animals
____
____
____

4 decide to go to Yosemite / see bears and giant trees
____
____

5 go to California / not see any whales
____
____

6 have time / also like to climb Mount Whitney
____
____

2 ▶ Verbs with 'up'

Complete the sentences. Use the correct form of one of the verbs in the box and up.

cut • go • grow • look
pick • put • shut • wake **+ up**

1 I've never ________ this tent *up* before. Can you help me?
2 We bought a tent three years ago. Prices have ____________ a lot since then.
3 Dave is sleeping again. ________ him ____ !
4 Do you know the number of the Park Office?
– No, but we can ________ it ____ .
5 Can you ____________ that wood? We want to make a fire.
6 I've dropped my knife. Can you ________ it ____ ?
7 The boys in the next tent are so noisy. When are they going to ____________ ?
8 The boys are like babies sometimes. They should ____________ .

We put the tents up by a river.

3 ▶ Later that night

Some of the group had problems that night.
Complete the conversations in the tents with gerunds *from the box on the right. You can use some of them more than once.*

being • camping • getting • looking • meeting • raining • seeing • sleeping

__________ is great.

I enjoy __________ in the country.

I love __________ in a tent.

I'm scared of __________ a ghost.

I'm looking forward to __________ in my own bed again.

I'm fed up with __________ at the rain.

I'm going to dream about __________ bears.

When will it stop __________?

__________ is difficult.

I miss __________ in my bed.

I hate __________ wet.

4 ▶ Questions

One of the group met a very friendly park ranger, Julie.
What questions did Julie ask?

Julie, the park ranger

1 *Where* __________ *from?*
I come from Britain.

2 *Have* __________ *before?*
No, this is my first time in the USA.

3 *Are* __________
Yes, I'm having a wonderful stay.

4 *How long* __________ ?
We've been here since last Friday.

5 __________
Yes, my tent is very nice, but my sleeping bag is too warm.

6 __________
No, we haven't seen any bears, but we saw some bear tracks yesterday.

7 __________
We go walking or cycling every day, and we've been swimming once.

8 __________
In the lake. The water was very cold!

4 New York – Gateway to America

1 ▶ Immigrants

a *Complete this network about immigrants.*

Immigrants

They all hope for …
- a b_______r life

When they arrive they have to …
- find a place to l____e
- find w____k
- learn a new l__________ge
- go through the i_________________n process

They leave their own countries because of …
- p______________n
- h________r
- p________y

On the journey to the new country they feel …
- s__d
- wo______d
- ex ______d
- ner______s

b *Complete these tables.*

noun	adjective
danger	*dangerous*
religion	______________
poverty	______________
hunger	______________
thirst	______________
freedom	______________

noun	verb
immigration	______________
hope	______________
decision	______________
life	______________

p. 55

2 REVISION The journey to America

Put the verbs in the simple past.

Many immigrants to America (not, want) *didn't want* to leave their own countries. They (leave) _______ because of persecution or poverty. The journey to America (be) _______ exciting for some people. But many (feel) _______ sad or nervous. When people (decide) _____________ to leave home, they (have to) ___________ say goodbye to their families and friends and sometimes they (not, see) ________________ them again. Life in America (not, be) ____________ easy for immigrants. Many of them (not, know) __________________ any English. They (not, have) _________________ much money and they only (bring) _____________ a few things with them from home. But they (be) _______ all ready to work hard and they (hope) ___________ for a better life in a free country.

3 **REVISION** Before Daniel's bar mitzvah

Write sentences. Use the present perfect.

1 Daniel's mum (find) ________________ his great-grandfather's prayer shawl.

2 Daniel (not, learn) ____________________ his piece from the Torah.

3 'Daniel, (you, write, yet) ______________________ the cards ______ ?'

4 'Why (you, not, put) ______________________ a stamp on this card, dear?'

5 Lots of people (already, answer) ______________________________ the invitations.

6 'We (not, ask, yet) ____________________ aunt Sarah for the camcorder ______ .'

4 ▶ What do you think?

Add the *only where you need it.*

1 a 'What do you think of _______ rap music?'

b 'I liked ______ programme about rap last night.'

2 a 'Look at _______ dolphins. Aren't they great?'

b 'Do you know that ______ dolphins are in great danger?'

3 a 'I believe that we must stop _______ pollution at once.'

b 'Isn't _____ pollution of the river terrible?'

4 a 'I love _______ spaghetti.'

b '______ spaghetti my dad makes is fantastic.'

p. 57/A3

5 ▶ What do you enjoy?

Fill in the *where you need the article.*

1 'Do you like reading _____ computer magazines?'

– 'Sometimes. There were some interesting articles in _____ last magazine I read.'

2 'Did you watch _____ film *The Beach* on TV last night?'

– 'No, I don't like watching _____ films like that.'

3 'My brother loves watching _____ car races.'

– 'Did he watch _____ race at Silverstone yesterday?'

4 'I don't like _____ hot weather.'

– 'Really? I love going on holiday to _____ hot places.'

5 'Have you ever dreamt of making _____ music?'

– 'Yes, I have. I really love _____ music of the sixties.'

6 'My mother enjoys going to _____ museums very much.'

– 'My mother enjoys going to _____ rock concerts most of all.'

p. 57/A3

Just for fun

Why does the Statue of Liberty stand in New York Harbor?
Because it can't sit down.

6 BLUE BOX will-future + going to → blue box, p.135

a *These people want to help. What can they say? Use the* will-future.

1 I can't remember what this word means.

I'll look it up for you.

2 This bike is so heavy.

____

3 I can't find the bus station on this map.

____

4 I can't clean the top of the window. It's too high.

____

5 I can't find my favourite trousers anywhere.

____

tip Sometimes you decide, promise or offer sth. to sb. spontaneously[1]. Then you use **will**, e.g. *I'm thirsty – I'll make you some tea.*
Sometimes you think about something and plan it. Then you use **going to**, e.g. *I'm going to make you a lovely meal tomorrow.*

[1] spontaneously [spɒn'teɪnɪəslɪ] spontan

b *These people have lots of plans. What are they saying? Use* going to.

(you, stay) Are you going to stay at home this summer?

– No, we (go) ______________ go to France.

What (you, do) ______________ this afternoon?

– I (look) ______________ for some sports shoes in town.

I (not, buy) ______________ a car. They're too boring.

I (buy) ______________ a motorbike.

I (not, go out) ______________ this evening. Dad (cook) ______________ a special meal because it's mum's birthday.

p. 57/A3

7 ▶ Help the tourist

Complete the conversation.

TOURIST Excuse me. I want to go to the town hall. Where do I have to get off?

DRIVER Was sagt sie?

YOU Sie möchte wissen, wo sie aussteigen muss ______________.

DRIVER Nächste Haltestelle.

YOU The driver says You must get off the bus at the next stop.

TOURIST Where do I go then?

YOU The town hall is opposite the bus stop.

DRIVER Das Rathaus ist gegenüber von der Haltestelle.

YOU She says thank you. ______________.

TOURIST Thank you so much.

p. 58/A5
+ p.86

8 ▶ Another name for New York

Complete the puzzle to find out another name for New York.

1 The borough north of Manhattan
2 Brooklyn Bridge goes across it.
3 The name of an airport and a high school
4 Here you can buy whatever you want to.
5 The biggest park in New York
6 The ... State Building
7 This borough has the largest population.
8 The most exciting square in New York.

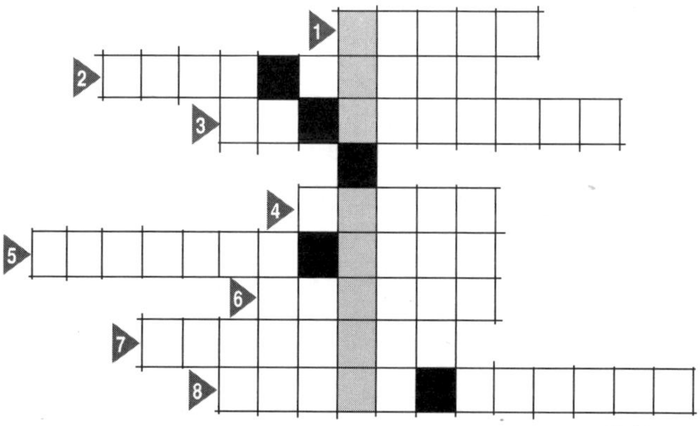

p. 58/A6

9 ▶ What really happened?

Tick the right picture.

1 If it hadn't rained,
I wouldn't have got wet.

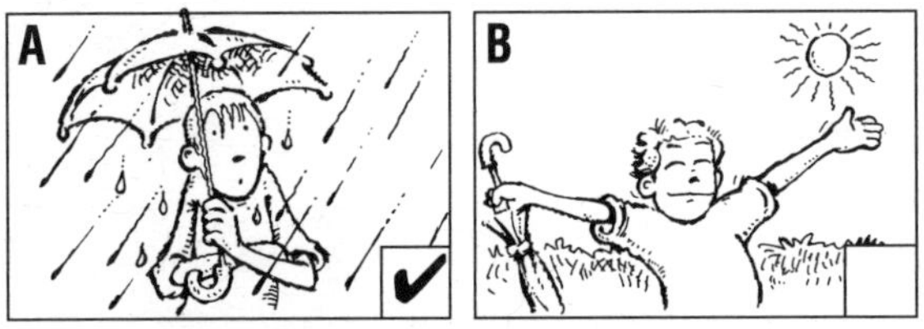

2 If my friend had phoned,
I would have gone out last night.

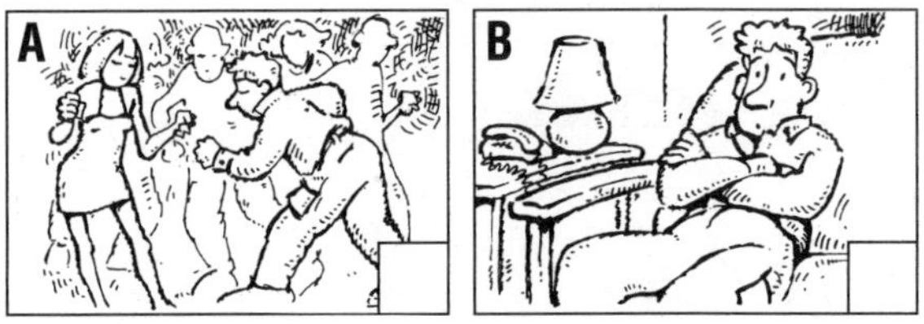

3 If I had forgotten the milk,
Dad would have been fed up.

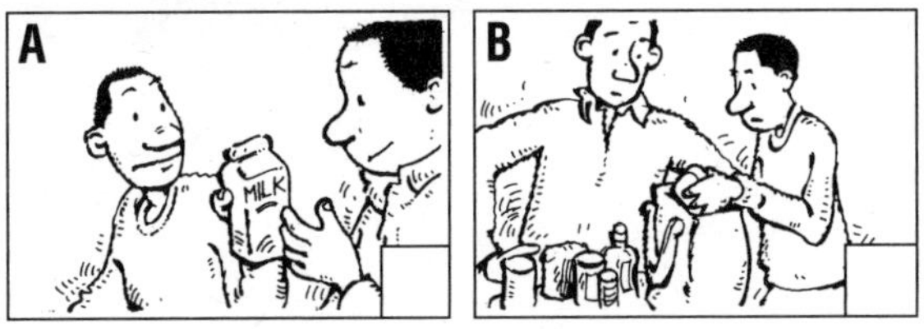

4 If I hadn't caught my brother,
he would have hurt himself.

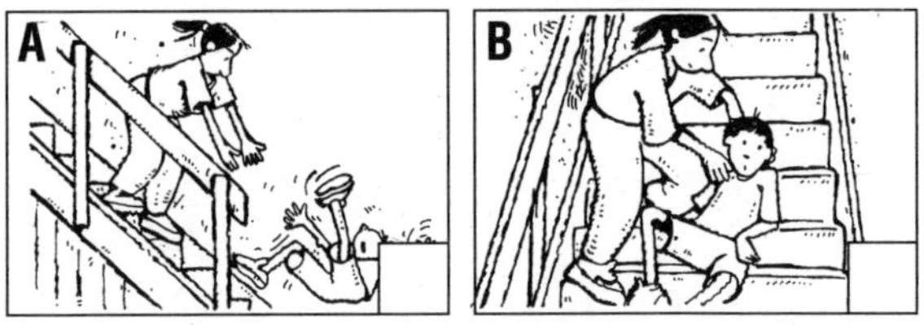

5 If the music hadn't been so loud,
I would have heard the phone.

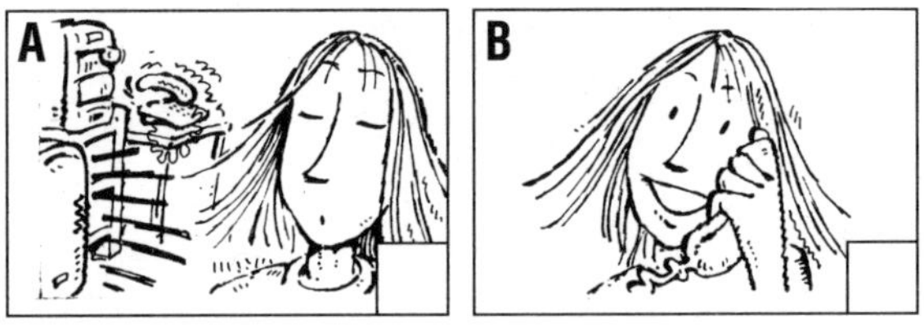

p. 60/A10

10 ▶ What would have happened?

Complete these sentences.
Use the ideas on the right.

would wouldn't	have	won the race lost it worried gone to the cinema caught the bus stopped

1 I had trouble with my best friend. We didn't go to the cinema.

If I hadn't had trouble with my best friend, we *would have gone to the cinema.*

2 I didn't win the race. I didn't start my training early enough.

If I had started my training early enough, I ________________________________ .

3 I've lost my cinema ticket. I didn't put it in my pocket.

If I had put my cinema ticket in my pocket, I ________________________________ .

4 I didn't get up early enough. I didn't catch the bus.

If I had got up early enough, I ________________________________ .

5 I didn't shout. The car didn't stop.

If I had shouted, the car ________________________________ .

6 I didn't phone mum. She worried.

If I had phoned mum, she ________________________________ .

▶▶▶ NOW YOU

Finish the sentences and use would have + past participle.

1 If I had been young in the 1970s, ______________________________.

2 If I had lived five hundred years ago, ______________________________.

3 If I had been more careful, ______________________________.

4 If I had gone to the party last night, ______________________________.

5 If I had forgotten my best friend's birthday, ______________________________.

p. 60/A10

WORKING WITH THE TEXT

11 ▶ The Shapiros' day

The notes below are about the Shapiros' day in New York.

a *Draw in arrows (→) to show the correct order of the boxes.*

b *Retell the story in your exercise book with the help of the notes. You can add other details you find important.*

tip Don't forget to use linking words and time words.
Linking words: *after, and, as, because, before, but, or, so, when.*
Time words: *after that, at first, later, one day, suddenly, then.*

		the Shapiro family – leave Minerva – go to New York City – Daniel's bar mitzvah party
take the bus – visit – Statue of Liberty – first – ride through Midtown – great – take – boat trip – Staten Island ferry – back at Battery Park	the Shapiros – go – a coffee shop on 42nd Street – have breakfast – see – Statue of Liberty – UN Building – Empire State Building ...	on their way to New York – Mr Shapiro – have a bad dream – bag lady – street gang – wake up – bus driver – shout – 42nd Street Station
the Shapiros – have a cup of coffee at deli – Mr Shapiro – shocked – see – an old bag lady – look like the woman in his dream	take the subway to Empire State Building – downstairs – see – a crazy-looking man	crazy man – explain – meaning of 'Big Apple' – jazz musicians – play their gigs – New York City – biggest apple
shopping at Macy's – the Shapiros – go – West 68th – have great fun at Daniel's bar mitzvah party	on the way down – Mr Shapiro – notice – wallet – missing – think – 'black guy' – shocked – crazy-looking man – give – wallet	Mr Shapiro – embarrassed – take the elevator – to 102nd floor – top of Empire State Building – fantastic

pp. 65–68

12 ▶ ... discuss your day out in English

Sage, dass du den Central Park sehen möchtest.

___

Sage, dass es dir egal ist und schlage vor, mit dem Bus zu fahren.

___

Sage, dass es mit der U-Bahn schneller geht.

___

Sage, dass ihr nachher den Broadway besuchen könntet.

___

Sage, dass du lieber bei Macy's einkaufen würdest.

___

13 ▶ ... complete the expressions

Use the words in the box.

She made • Don't let • What's
She's going to take • You have to get

1 ___ | an exam. / a photo.

2 ___ | the matter? / up?

3 ___ | a brilliant speech. / a good decision.

4 ___ | me down. / him take the map.

5 ___ | ready. / off at the next stop.

14 ▶ ... write about a family celebration

Write about a special family party.

What kind of party was it?
Where was it?
Who came?
Did everybody wear special clothes?
Did someone make a speech?
Was it boring or funny?
Was there music?
Did people dance?
Did you enjoy it?

___

Unit 4 How to use a dictionary (English-German)

1 ▶ Getting to know your dictionary

a *The* running heads *on this page are:* __________ *and* __________.

b *Find the short forms of these grammar words on the page.*

Adjektiv: ______________

Adverb: ______________

Pronomen: ______________

Objekt: ______________

c *Find two grammar words that haven't got short forms.*

____

____

d *Look at the phonetic symbols. Find one word for each symbol.*

ɪ *nibble*

aɪ ______________

iː ______________

θ ______________

əʊ ______________

e *Find one English word with two German meanings.*

__________ 1 ______________

2 ______________

f *What's the* adverb *form of these* adjectives?

The child asked (nice) ________.

They played (noisy) __________.

g *Find these short forms on the page. What do they mean?*

BE

____

umgs

____

nibble 186 **none**

wonder what will happen next. Ich frage mich, was als Nächstes passieren wird. **It was years until I next saw her.** Bis ich sie das nächste Mal sah, vergingen Jahre.
▲ **ˌnext-ˈbest** *Adj* nächstbeste(r,s)

nibble /ˈnɪbl/ *Verb* knabbern

nice /naɪs/ *Adj* **1** angenehm, schön, gut **Have a nice day!** Einen schönen Tag! **You look very nice today.** Du siehst heute sehr hübsch aus. **This doesn't taste very nice.** Das schmeckt nicht besonders gut.
2 nett
◆ **nice and …** (*umgs*) schön … **It's nice and warm by the fire.** Es ist schön warm am Kamin.

nicely /ˈnaɪsli/ *Adv* **1** nett **You can have a biscuit if you ask nicely.** Du bekommst einen Keks, wenn du nett fragst.
2 (*umgs*) sehr gut **This flat will suit us nicely.** Diese Wohnung wird uns vollauf genügen.

nick /nɪk/ *Verb + Obj* (*BE*) (*Slang*) **1** klauen
2 nick sb (for sth) jdn (für etwas) einsperren

nickel /ˈnɪkl/ *Nomen* **1** Nickel
2 Fünfcentstück

nickname /ˈnɪkneɪm/ *Nomen* Spitzname

nicotine /ˈnɪkətiːn/ *Nomen* Nikotin

niece /niːs/ *Nomen* Nichte

night /naɪt/ *Nomen* **1** Nacht **Why don't you stay the night?** Willst du nicht über Nacht bleiben? **Owls come out at night.** Eulen werden nachts munter.
2 Abend **Let's go out on Saturday night.** Lass uns Samstagabend ausgehen. **8 o'clock at night** 8 Uhr abends **I tried to phone Nigel last night.** Ich habe gestern Abend versucht, Nigel anzurufen.
◆ **have an early/a late night** früh/spät ins Bett gehen **good night** gute Nacht
▲ **ˈnightdress** *Nomen* Nachthemd **ˈnight school** *Nomen* Abendschule **ˈnight-time** *Nomen, kein Plural* Nacht

nightie /ˈnaɪti/ *Nomen* (*umgs*) Nachthemd

nightly /ˈnaɪtli/ **1** *Adj* allabendlich, allnächtlich
2 *Adv* jeden Abend, jede Nacht

nightmare /ˈnaɪtme… N… n A…traum

ninth[1] /naɪnθ/ *Pronom, Adj* neunte(r,s) ☛ Anwendungsbeispiele für Zahlwörter stehen unter **sechste(r,s)**.

ninth[2] /naɪnθ/ *Pronom, Nomen* Neuntel

nip /nɪp/ *Verb* (ni**pp**ing, ni**pp**ed, ni**pp**ed) **1** zwicken
2 *ohne Obj* (*umgs*) flitzen **She nipped round to the shop.** Sie ging kurz zum Laden.

nitrate /ˈnaɪtreɪt/ *Nomen* Nitrat

nitrogen /ˈnaɪtrədʒən/ *Nomen* Stickstoff

no[1] /nəʊ/ *Adj* kein **No two days are the same.** Kein Tag ist wie der andere. **He's no friend of mine.** Er ist kein Freund von mir. **No smoking.** Rauchen verboten.
◆ **no way** (*umgs*) auf keinen Fall
▲ **ˈno one** *Pronom* niemand, keiner **No one else was there.** Sonst war niemand da.

no[2] /nəʊ/ *Adv* nicht **Alice is feeling no better this morning.** Alice fühlt sich heute früh nicht besser. **no later than 31st July** bis spätestens 31. Juli

no[3] /nəʊ/ *Ausruf* nein ☛ Hinweis bei **nein**.

nobility /nəʊˈbɪləti/ *Nomen* Adel

noble[1] /ˈnəʊbl/ *Adj* **1** edel, hochherzig
2 adlig

noble[2] /ˈnəʊbl/ *Nomen* Adlige

nobly /ˈnəʊbli/ *Adv* edelmütig

nobody /ˈnəʊbədi/ *Pronom* niemand, keiner **He screamed but nobody came to help him.** Er schrie, aber niemand kam ihm zu Hilfe. **There was nobody at home.** Keiner war zu Hause.

nocturnal /nɒkˈtɜːnl/ *Adj* **1** nächtlich
2 (*Tiere*) Nacht-

nod[1] /nɒd/ *Verb* (no**dd**ing, no**dd**ed, no**dd**ed) nicken **Nod your head if you understand me.** Nicken Sie mit dem Kopf, wenn Sie mich verstehen.

nod[2] /nɒd/ *Nomen* Nicken

noise /nɔɪz/ *Nomen* Geräusch, Lärm **Try not to make a noise.** Bemüh dich, keinen Lärm zu machen. **Why is the engine making so much noise?** Warum ist der Motor so laut?

noisy /ˈnɔɪzi/ *Adj* (**noisier, noisiest**) (*Adv* **noisily**) lärmend, laut ☛ Hinweis bei **laut**.

no…inate … **…minate sb/sth**

2 ▶ Dictionary practice

Use your own dictionary and find the best German translation for the underlined words.

Fiorello Henry LaGuardia was a <u>well-known</u> American in the 1930s and 1940s. He was <u>raised</u> in Arizona, but moved to Italy as a young man. When he returned to the US he worked <u>temporarily</u> on Ellis Island as an <u>interpreter</u>. Later he <u>entered politics</u> and in 1933 he became mayor[1] of New York City. He was very popular and for a long time he <u>ran</u> his own radio programme. He did lots of good things for New York. For example, in 1936 he <u>founded</u> the LaGuardia High School of Music and Art. Today one of New York's airports is <u>named after him</u>.

[1] mayor [meə(r)] *Bürgermeister/in*

1 ______________ 2 ______________

3 ______________ 4 ______________

5 ______________

6 ______________ 7 ______________

8 ______________

5 Nebraska – the Middle of Nowhere?

1 ▶ The big school crossword puzzle

Complete this puzzle.

Down

1 A kind of school in the USA
2 Sort of Maths
3 Another word for lesson
4 What you learn
6 Another word for pupil
8 Physics, Chemistry and Biology
11 The time when you can eat at school
13 Group of students at school
14 An American word for form

Across

5 Cupboard at school for your things
7 A school year has three of these
9 You can surf the Internet with it
10 Time for your homework at school
12 A place where people go to learn
15 Room or building for books
16 Another word for test at the end of the school year
17 An American word for timetable
18 Person who gives lessons

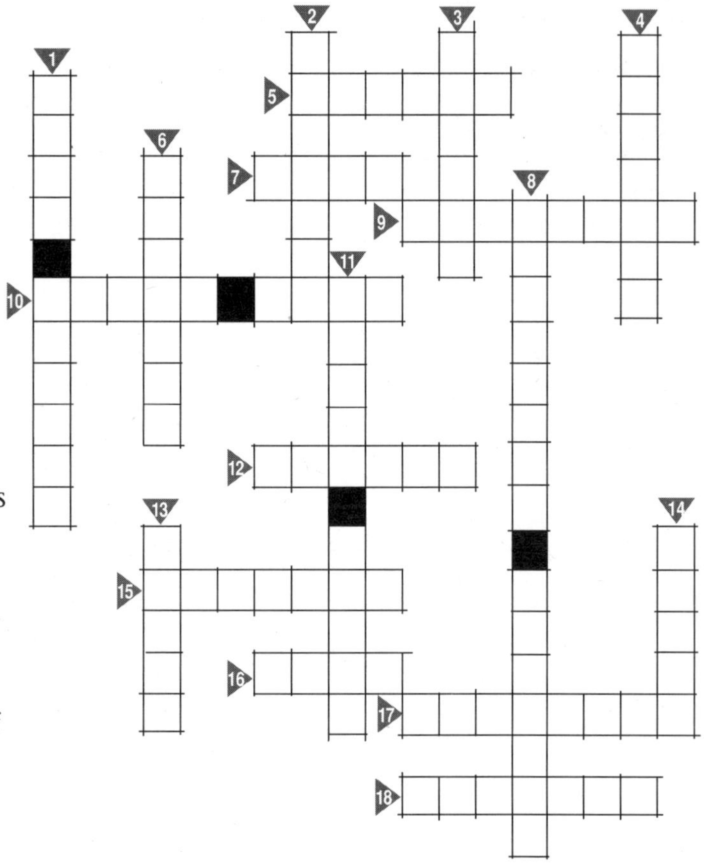

p. 71

2 REVISION At school

Answer these questions and use adverbs *like* never, usually, sometimes, often, always.

1 How do you get to school?
I usually go to school by bus.
2 How long does it take you to get to school?

____

3 Do you have lunch at school?

____

4 Where do you do your homework?

____

5 How often do you forget things for school?

____

6 What kind of clothes do you wear for school?

____

3 ▶ BLUE BOX Any ideas? → blue box, p. 139

Complete these sentences and use words like any, anybody, anything, anywhere, *etc.*

1 Do you know *any* good jokes?

2 When I have finished my homework I can do ______________ I want.

3 I'm so hungry I'd eat ______________.

4 Is there ______________ I can leave my bike?

5 ______________ can see that that's wrong.

6 You can take ______________ bus from here.

It's your birthday? Cook anything you want for dinner.

p. 72/A1

4 ▶ Word snake

a *How many* past participles *can you find?*

minosoldfetputaserehurtefsshownfguedrunkfgbtpaidersuztuhearddeaewmseentfgbuiltgfgtspentgetur

b *Write down the three forms of all the verbs you've found.*

sell sold sold ______________

____

____

____

p. 72/A2

5 ▶ Computer games

a *Complete the network. Use the verbs in the box in the* passive.

copy • develop • play
produce • sell • swap

b *Can you add more verbs?*

p. 72/A2

6 ▶ The Model-T – America's most successful car

Complete the text. Use the passive *in the* simple past.

The first Ford car (build) *was built* behind Henry Ford's home in Detroit in 1896. In 1908 the first Model-Ts (sell) ______________ . They quickly became famous because they were cheap and easy to drive. The Model-T (call) ______________ the 'Tin Lizzie'. More than 15 million Model-Ts (build) ______________ in Detroit and Highland Park, Michigan. The car (also, produce) ______________ ______________ in factories in Europe. In 1913 the world's first assembly line[1] for cars (build) ______________ . Because of this, the price went down from $850 in 1908 to less than $300 in 1925. The workers got $5 for an 8-hour day.

The Model-T was so popular that it (also, use) ______________ for work on farms. In 1927 the new Model-A (develop) ______________ and the last Model-Ts (produce) ______________ .

[1] assembly line [ə'sembli] *Fließband(montage)*

p. 73/A5

7 ▶ MADD – facts about young people and alcohol

Complete the facts about young people in the USA and alcohol with the passive *of the verbs.*

1 Among young people alcohol (use) ______________ more often than any other drug.
2 Every year many young drivers (kill) ______________ because of drunk driving.
3 In 1999 one teenager an hour (kill) ______________ every weekend in a car crash.
4 Almost 50 % of these crashes (cause) ______________ because of drunk driving.
5 At college more money (spent) ______________ on alcohol than on all other drinks.

▶▶▶ NOW YOU

Answer these questions.

Is drunk driving a problem with young people in Germany?

____

____

What do you do when someone has drunk too much and wants to drive you home?

____

____

p. 73/A5

8 ▶ Famous people

Complete the sentences. Use the verbs below.

design • discover • invent • sing • write

1 Penicillin *was discovered* by ____________________.

2 The telephone ____________________
by ____________________.

3 The Golden Gate Bridge ____________________
____________________.

4 'Ebony and Ivory' ____________________
____________________.

5 'Anita and Me' ____________________
____________________.

p. 74/A6

[9] ▶ This can be done easily

Use the passive *with* can *in these sentences.*

1 Teacher to class: 'Paper (recycle, easily) *can* easily *be recycled*.'

2 Shop assistant to customer: 'This mobile phone (use) ____________ abroad.'

3 Sign at tourist information: Come to our zoo! It (visit) ____________ every day from 10 am to 6 pm.'

4 Newsreader on TV: 'Tonight the Space Shuttle (see) ____________ in the clear sky.'

5 Father to son: 'I can't work because of your loud music. It (hear) ____________ all over the house.

p. 74/A7

10 ▶ Translating

Translate this message on a school notice board. Write the translation in your exercise book. Look at the green box on page 88 for help.

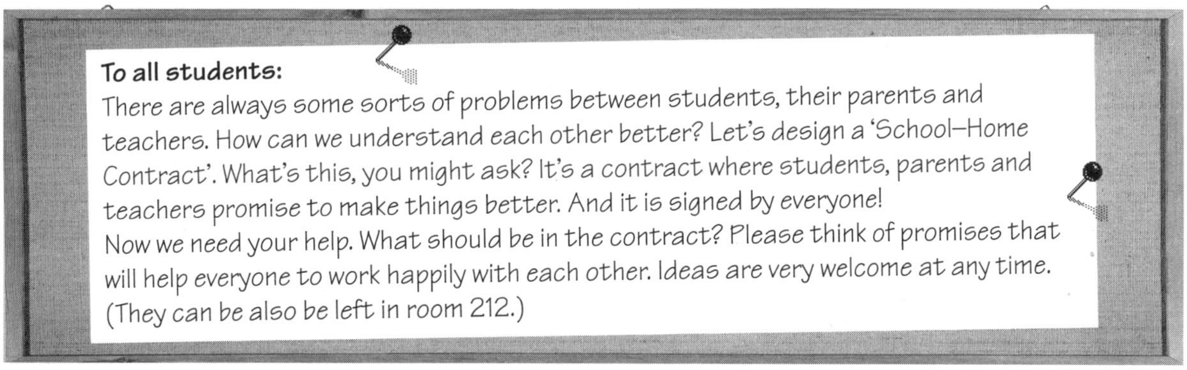

To all students:
There are always some sorts of problems between students, their parents and teachers. How can we understand each other better? Let's design a 'School–Home Contract'. What's this, you might ask? It's a contract where students, parents and teachers promise to make things better. And it is signed by everyone!
Now we need your help. What should be in the contract? Please think of promises that will help everyone to work happily with each other. Ideas are very welcome at any time. (They can be also be left in room 212.)

▶▶▶ NOW YOU

Would you find this kind of contract useful? What would you like to see in this contract? Write some promises in your exercise book.

I promise that I will … / to …

p. 75/A10

WORKING WITH THE TEXT

11 ▶ Describing people

a *Complete the words below. Use your dictionary if you need help. Add more words if you can.*

What people can look like

t__ll
th__n
b____________l
o__d

sh____t
d____k
pr____y
y______g

What people can be like

nice
k____d
f_________ly

successful
bu__y
cl______r
in____________t
r___h

wild
f___n
cr____y
si___y
n____sy

horrible
r____ ist
ru____
v_________t

un_____r
str____t

miserable
s____y
ne________s
unl______y

b Find more words in the text on pages 80–81 for the network.

____

____

c Describe Laura or Mike in your exercise book.

12 ▶ A diary entry

Imagine you are Janine or Melanie. Choose one of them and write a diary entry about the scene in the library. What do you think about Laura now? Do you understand her? Will you still be friends with her? Do you think differently about Mike now? Will you talk to Laura about Mike again?

My diary

____

____

____

____

____

____

____

____

____

pp. 80–82

Unit 5 NOW YOU CAN ...

13 ▶ ... talk about a date

How do you say these things in English?

1 Sage, dass du eine Verabredung mit Tina/Tino hast *(or choose a name)*.

____

2 Sage, dass du sie/ihn abholen wirst.

____

3 Sage, dass ihr vereinbart habt, ins Kino zu gehen.

____

____

4 Sage, dass es dir egal ist, ob sich Tom mit Jenny trifft.

____

5 Sage, dass du Tom grüßen lässt.

____

14 ▶ ... use the correct prepositions with verbs

a *Put these verbs in the table so that they go with the right preposition:*

lie care react ask pay attention talk listen worry

lie, ______________________________ ______________________________	to
care, ______________________________ ______________________________	about

b *Can you add to the lists?*

15 ▶ ... write about school

What do you like about American high schools? What do you like better at your German school?

Write about
- lessons and subjects
- homework
- where you eat
- activities at school
- classroom
- timetable
- lockers
- how you get to school

____

____

____

____

____

____

____

____

____

Revision (Units 4–5)

1 ▶ A terrible week

Debbie has had a terrible week. Complete the text.

On Monday I failed my Social Studies quiz. If I (do) *had done* more work the night before, I (pass) ______________ . If I (not, go) ______________ to that party on Saturday night, I (not, feel) ______________ so tired on Sunday. On Monday evening dad forgot to pick me up from band practice. If I (call) ______________ him, he (not, forget) ______________ . On Wednesday night I got home really late and mom was mad. I was only at grandma's. If I (tell) ______________ her where I was going, she (not, be) ______________ so mad. I wanted to go to a movie on Friday, but I didn't have any money. I'd left all my money in the pocket of my jeans. Dad washed them and the money got wet. If I (take) ______________ the money out, it (not, get) ______________ . Dad offered me some money, but I decided it was safer to stay at home.

2 ▶ The school newspaper

a *Bobby works for the Sutton High School newspaper. Read the interview with him.*

TOM How many people work on the newspaper?
BOBBY About six people do most of the work.
TOM What do you do first?
BOBBY Well, first we need some articles. Different people write them and send them to our office. Then I sit down with some other people and we choose the best ones.
TOM What about photos?
BOBBY Students take the pictures we need. When it's all ready we sell the newspaper in school. Quite a lot of people buy it!

b *Finish this report for the school website about Bobby's newspaper. Use the* simple present passive.

Sutton School on the Net

THE SCHOOL NEWSPAPER – DID YOU KNOW?

Most of the work ______________ . First of all, the articles ______________ . Then the best articles ______________ . The photos ______________ .
The newspaper ______________ .
You should buy it too – it's good!

3 ▶ New York, New York

Complete the sentences. Use the verbs in the box in the passive – simple present *or* simple past.

bring • build • find • hurt
sell • speak • take • visit

1 There was an accident on the subway yesterday. Ten people *were hurt* and two people ________________ away in an ambulance.

2 The Empire State Building ________________ by 3.8 million people every year.

3 How many languages ________________ in New York?

4 If you want a cheap ticket to the theatre, go to the ticket office just before the play starts. Sometimes tickets ________________ at cheap prices.

5 This museum sounds exciting. It says in the brochure: History ________________ to life. – That's what they all say!

6 Ask the guides anything you like: 'When _______ this building ___________?', 'Who was born here?' They know everything.

7 Something bad happened to my friend in New York. His bag ________________ from his hotel room. It ________________ later, but the thieves had taken all his money.

The Big USA Quiz

You know a lot about the USA. Probably more than you think! Try this quiz and test yourself. On the right are page numbers so that you can look for the information in your pupil's book.

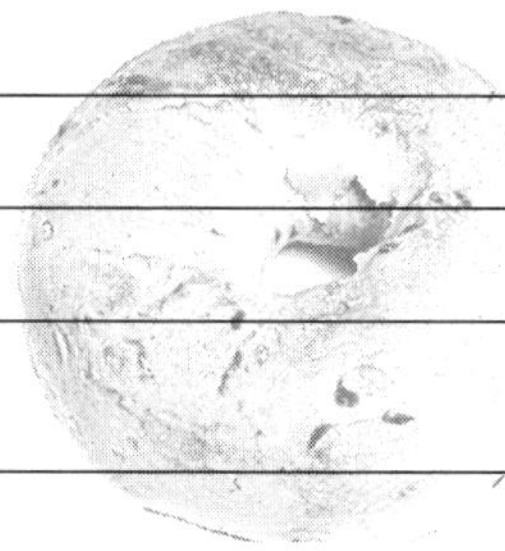

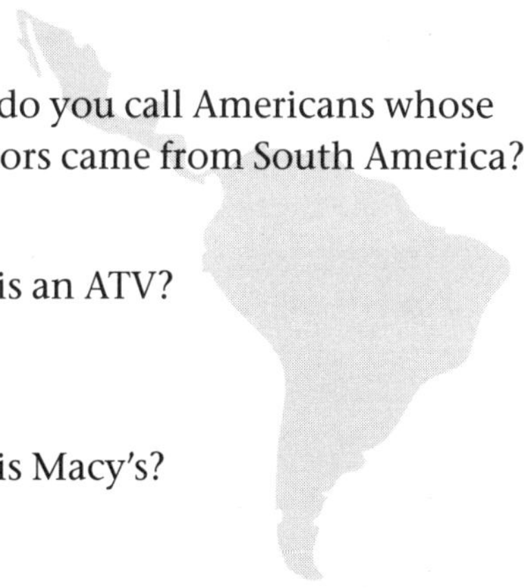

		Page
1 How long have the Inuits been in Alaska?	a) ☐ about 800 years b) ☐ about 8000 years c) ☐ about 80,000 years	30
2 How many boroughs are there in New York?	________________	58
3 Name one New York borough.	________________	58/105
4 Name two animals that you find in Alaska.	________________	28
5 What are tacos?	________________	12
6 What can you buy in a deli?	________________ ________________	67
7 What do you call Americans whose ancestors came from South America?	________________	122
8 What is an ATV?	a) ☐ a vehicle b) ☐ a TV programme c) ☐ a movie studio	33
9 What is Macy's?	a) ☐ a theatre b) ☐ a hotel c) ☐ a department store	58

Page

10 What date is Independence Day in the USA? 53
a) ☐ February 14
b) ☐ July 4
c) ☐ October 31

11 What is New York sometimes called? ____________________ 67

12 What is special about the Alaskan summer? ____________________ 26

13 What is the BE word for:
a) sidewalk? ____________________ 10
b) pants? ____________________ 17
c) French fries? ____________________ 17
d) downtown? ____________________ 133
e) subway? ____________________ 17

14 What is the capital of Alaska? 30
a) ☐ Anchorage
b) ☐ Juneau
c) ☐ Barrow

15 What were the 49ers looking for? ____________________ 43

16 What's the highest mountain in the USA? ____________________ 28

17 What's the population of the USA? 13
a) ☐ about 27 million
b) ☐ about 270 million
c) ☐ about 720 million

18 When did the blacks become free in the USA? 61
a) ☐ 1805
b) ☐ 1865
c) ☐ 1965

19 Where did poor immigrants to the USA land? ____________________ 54

20 Which is bigger? 104
a) ☐ Germany
b) ☐ California

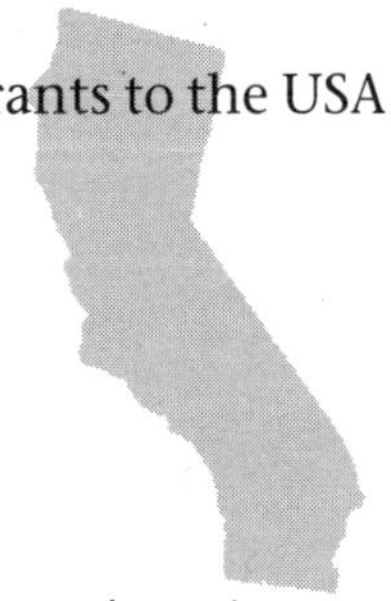

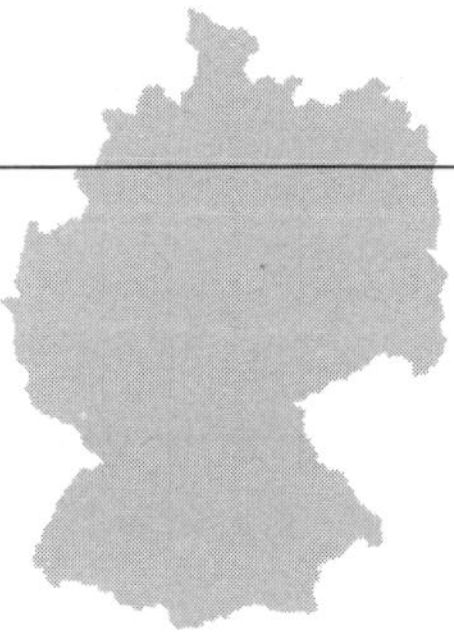

22 Which mark is better in an American school? 73
a) ☐ A
b) ☐ F

23 Which US state is known as the 'Sunshine State'? ____________________ 9